MORGAN & ME

ISBN: 978-1-910131-66-4

First published in 2020 by Happen*Stance* Press
21 Hatton Green, Glenrothes KY7 4SD
https://happenstancepress.com

Printed and bound by Imprint Digital, Exeter
https://digital.imprint.co.uk

MORGAN & ME

A Memoir

Hamish Whyte

HAPPENSTANCE PRESS

Contents

Friendship may be born of affinities, but it lives with mysteries.

—Barbara Taylor

I love memoir, its generosity, at once elegy and Thank You.
And of course a side serving of self-knowledge.

—Andrew Greig

To Lel Verth
in friendship

1. Prologue: Two Pieces of Paper

I'm sitting looking at two pieces of detritus from my personal archives—an old piece of paper with biro-scribbled handwriting, and a membership card.

The tiny, greenish-blue, pasteboard membership card is a relic of the Glasgow University Alexandrian Society, Session 1968-69. In October 1968, I was twenty-one and commencing the final year of my four-year degree in Classics. I'd just started going out with Winifred, who worked in the University Library (and whom I would marry two years later). I didn't know what I wanted to do career-wise except write poems and not teach. I liked Greek better than Latin and was translating Sappho. The Alexandrian Society was a venerable one, then in its eighty-second year.

The names of the society's office-bearers are printed on the back of the card. I'm listed as one of two vice-presidents along with Miss Morna Thomas (where is she now?). The year's programme gets off to a good start with the Opening Night 'Mr. Edwin G. Morgan, M. A. *What are we to do with Aristophanes?*' I have no memory of what we were to do with Aristophanes, but I do remember my fleeting impression of Mr. Edwin G. Morgan—an English Department lecturer who dared to speak to us Classics students about Greek Comedy!

We knew nothing about the English Department nor did I really want to. However, this chap from English was youngish-seeming (though he was forty-eight at the time), with Buddy-Holly-type spectacles. He was erudite and, above all, enthusiastic. I had no inkling he was also a poet—I believe he kept quiet about it in his own department—until the following year when I picked up my friend Irving's copy of Morgan's new collection, his second book, *The Second Life*. Irving was a medical student but he read and wrote poetry—and recommended the author. The book was fascinating. It had been typeset by computer and included concrete poems printed on differently coloured paper. Years later (after finally meeting Eddie) I was ferreting through his box files for my bibliography of his work and came across the very typescript of his talk on Aristophanes. I vividly remember the frisson of recognition.

The second item in front of me as I write is a rather grubby piece of paper, the bottom half of a lined foolscap sheet from the kind of notepad I used for lecture notes at university. It's much creased from folding, and onto it I've transcribed (probably with my then favoured yellow Bic black ink fine ballpoint, in very crabbed script, on both sides) the whole of Eddie's poem, 'The Fifth Gospel'. It was first published in *Scottish International*, 14 May 1971, from which I must have copied it.

Since reading John Robinson's *Honest to God* at school and taking a course in comparative religion at university, I'd been interested in radical or existential Christianity, including apocryphal gospel accounts and the quest for the historical Jesus (the greatest detective story). I imagine it was Eddie's poem's reversal of accepted sayings of Jesus that piqued my interest. Also, I'd always felt the words 'Render therefore unto Caesar the things which are Caesar's; and unto God the things' that are God's' (*Matthew* 22:21) was ironic, and meant (as in Eddie's version) 'Give nothing to Caesar, for nothing is Caesar's'. That is to say, everything is God's. It must have seemed important to me. (It occurs to me now that I've always been interested in reversals and turning things round; it's something I often do in poems—why, I don't know.) I must have carried this heretical poem about with me for some time for it to be in the state it is. And kept it.

So that was my introduction to Eddie and his work. And now the beginning of this memoir of my friendship with him. It was a literary as well as personal relationship, and consequently there will be much about books here—the literary and the personal intertwined. A memoir is perforce as much about its writer as the person remembered. Strangely, as someone whose poems routinely feature an 'I', I find it difficult to do a prose 'I'—it seems to be a different process: a process of revealing rather than concealment, of expanding rather than compression. It can be the opposite of writing poems. We shall see.

I've thought often about the phrase from Eddie's poem 'At Eighty': 'unknown is best'. Is it? I suppose I'm quite a timid person and the reticences of my suburban upbringing inhibit me from writing about some things. But I've just come across this passage from Stanley Kunitz's wonderful book about gardening and poetry, *The Wild Braid* (thank you, Brigid Collins, for putting me on to it):

> The mystery of the creative process is that the poem is there but *not* there within you, accumulating images. It needs to be released, but sometimes there are barriers. The poem incites fear; you are coming into truth in the writing of the poem, you are hesitant to explore unfamiliar areas [...] the path of the poem is through the unknown and even the unknowable, toward something for which you can find a language.

Now, that's encouraging. Maybe I could make writing prose like writing poems, not worry too much about the process, just try to let Morgan and me show through. On the surface, the terrain of my friendship with Eddie (thirty years, by my account) is more or less recoverable. What's underneath, however, is still to some extent unknown (because never considered deeply at the time, just lived) and will have to be mined, whether painfully or pleasurably. As Emily Dickinson wrote, 'It is true that the unknown is the largest need of the intellect though for it, no one thinks to thank God.' (Letter to Louise and Frances Norcross, August 1876).

So in the spirit of Eddie's constant exploration—and using as maps a motley collection of notes, diary entries, articles, conversations, postcards and letters (twelve boxes of them!) and dredged memories—I set out to navigate one of the most important relationships in my life.

August 29 1995 – 73 next week Squaw

012-086-24-3-1995

Dear Harold – Fruits & feathers!
—My Welsh visit this June took
us to Dafydd ap Gwilym's
grave, under a fascinating oak-like
yew-tree, suitably wild
split, impressive, innumerably
gnarled & furrowed to his
country.

I have been thinking about
your Nietzsche dazzling. My MSS
Trip to Milo are in OWL, so we
would have to the 1941 onwards.
It could be something like
'Stein in Venice' or 'Gist,'
or 'Seven American Poems', but
what about looking into
Cyprus? It's 150 pages, in
unbound sheets, mainly AM
but some PM too, mostly in
pencil but some in ink, signed
and dated April – June 1992.

It could make a good display
with something from the
production, plus the Concert
Jerome? How think you?
Off to Spring Friday, to
talk about sonnets, from
'Scotland,' from Shakespeare, from
Hopkins, from Milton, from
Elizabeth Barrett Browning —
and on to the species.

Forward, forward (seize the
cloak) —

Mller

2

2. Sustenance Provided: the Bibliographical Morgan

I might never have met Eddie if I hadn't become a librarian, and that was almost by accident. I had no real idea of where I wanted to go after university except be a poet in some way. I had enjoyed studying in libraries and wondered if a job surrounded by books would be just the thing. I was walking past the Mitchell Library in Glasgow one day and noticed that the library opened at 9.30 am. I thought that wasn't too early a start (after years of Greek lectures at 9.00 a.m.) so I wrote to the Head Librarian asking if there were any vacancies. I had never been in the Mitchell in my life, although it seemed a very grand place and pleasing to me as a fledgling book collector. As a reference library, it never lent books.

I was interviewed by the Depute City Librarian, Bill Alison, who told me he had a vision of public libraries becoming an all-graduate profession, and I was offered a post as a trainee librarian. And so I spent a year doing everything from menial tasks such as collating new books (that is, checking all the pages were there) to sorting old family papers in the Local History department, the Glasgow Room (under the guidance of the legendary Joe Fisher)—and getting married as well .

Then I went on to Strathclyde University to complete a post-graduate diploma in Librarianship. There I fell under the spell of Dr W. R. Aitken and his class on bibliography: the study of the history of printing and of book production (including, importantly, the editing process). This combined both my interest in writing and in history. As a poet, I had still not escaped from *White Goddess* country and, discovering the magisterial bibliography of Robert Graves by Fred Higginson, I embarked, rather arrogantly, on a continuation or updating of that work. This was to be my 'dissertation'.

I returned to the Mitchell (where my job had been kept open) not really wanting to be a librarian but a bibliographer. I loved the detective work involved in tracking down publications and also the listing and recording itself—the lure of not only books but 'about books'.

I was assigned to the Glasgow Room and began working on manuscripts, specifically the archives of the old Glasgow Grammar School (which later became Glasgow High School

and which Eddie attended in the 1930s). Calendaring, or cataloguing, manuscripts became just as fascinating as bibliographing—there's nothing like handwritten documents to
bring the past to life. Tea breaks were spent in the Magazine
Room, which seemed to have every periodical of the day (not
to mention the back numbers). I found myself with access to
a million books. I also began reading my way through the volumes in the local collection.

I discovered there was a thing that was Glasgow Crime Fiction and a thing that was Glasgow Poetry—and these became
my bibliographical obsessions. I embarked on a listing of all
books of crime fiction with some connection to Glasgow and
produced a typescript list of them for the library. In 1976 I also
produced the grandly titled *Glasgow Poets and Poetry: A Rep-
resentative Bibliography* 1950–1976. What was good about all
this was that I had the chance to read every literary magazine
published since the war, a period in which I saw the development of a recognisable group of Glasgow poets, from William
Montgomerie to Liz Lochhead. My introduction to the *Bibliography* made the modest claim that it was not complete but
might assist future research.

I have always had the view that research shouldn't be
wasted, so in the wake of this task, I set about putting together
an anthology of modern Glasgow poems, a tangible result of
my literary trawling—and, as far as I knew, it hadn't been done
before. I approached the poet and publisher Duncan Glen of
Akros Publications with the idea (he had previously accepted
some of my poems for his magazine). He was enthusiastic and
offered to publish it. This was my first anthology and as a nov-
ice I knew nothing about the drudgery of 'permissions'. Writing to poets such as Hugh MacDiarmid and Ian Hamilton Finlay seemed exciting (and sometimes was). As the Greeks said,
'through suffering we learn'.

Eddie, by this time, was an established poet with two major
collections under his belt and was approaching retirement
from the university. As a poet, I was still at early stages. My
first contact with Eddie himself was by letter, on 24 July 1977,
when I wrote asking permission to include some of his poems
in the Glasgow anthology. Unfortunately, this book foundered
through lack of funding, but a revised version was taken up

later by the Third Eye Centre in Glasgow and Glasgow Libraries who published it jointly in 1983 as *Noise and Smoky Breath: an illustrated anthology of Glasgow poems* 1900–1983.

So Eddie and I corresponded. Dear Mr Morgan. Dear Mr Whyte. He was happy about most of the poems being reprinted, but not so keen on having 'Northern Nocturnal' (from *New Poems* 1955) resurrected, although I felt it echoed Alexander Smith's great mid-nineteenth century poem 'Glasgow', from which the title of my anthology had been drawn. 'Northern Nocturnal' was eventually admitted to his *Collected Poems* of 1990. It's by no means uncommon for poets to dislike their early work being remembered—Norman MacCaig disowned his entirely. But Eddie grudgingly allowed me to use 'Night Pillion' from 1957, which describes a motor bike ride through Glasgow streets and which I thought anticipated his 1960s poems—both the city and the love poems:

> But tenements and lives, the wind, our wheels,
> The vibrant windshield and your guiding hands
> Fell into meaning, whatever meaning it was—
> Whatever joy it was

He offered some suggestions and I sent him a draft of the book contents. He replied: 'It looks as if it will be, overall, quite a strange and surprising book, which is as it should be, from the hilarious to the horrific with all steps in between.' This kind statement was immediately appropriated for the back cover—with permission, of course.

We continued to correspond about the anthology until May 1978. By then I thought it might well never happen at all. But I kept hopeful, and in 1980 the Third Eye Centre (now the Centre for Contemporary Arts) showed an interest in publishing it, possibly with illustrations.

Around this time the Mitchell Library was being extended, with a new building, on the site of the St Andrew's Halls, linked to the old one. New subject departments were established and I was appointed Senior Librarian in the Rare Books and Manuscripts Department.

I wrote to Eddie again on 5 April 1980, this time to let him know I was planning an exhibition to celebrate his sixtieth birthday (and his retirement as Titular Professor from the

University English Department). To accompany the display I intended to produce a selected bibliography of his work and wondered if I might 'pester him a little' with a few questions—such as, whether he was the Edwin Morgan who had written a study of Baudelaire, *Flowers of Evil*. I added that I hoped to compile a full bibliography in due course.

He replied, offering 'all the help I can'. He revealed that the 'Baudelaire is not mine, though it has been attributed to me so often ... I have almost come to believe I did write it.' He remembered one book dealer saying it 'threw an interesting light on Morgan's early religious development.'

In a later letter he passed on 'the sad facts about the late Edwin Morgan'—he had been an American poet and teacher: 'he left this sphere of things in 1957, age 59 ... R.I.P.!' He suggested we discuss the bibliography and that I 'come out here sometime and check on anything you have not seen.'

What he didn't realise was that he was offering me the Grail—a collector's, a bibliographer's, dream come true. As well as having been infected by the bibliography bug, I had caught the book-collecting disease some years earlier in my teens, haunting the barrows in Glasgow lanes and second-hand bookshops in Glasgow and Edinburgh. Compiling a bibliography seemed the logical outcome—and a useful justification, on the waste-not principle mentioned earlier—for collecting a favourite author, a step up from a straight catalogue.

We arranged a date, but it was put off by Eddie having a bad cold. I finally made my first visit on 22 April 1980. I arrived for an evening chat, pressing the steel button for 19 Whittinghame Court with some trepidation. I took the lift to the third floor and there he was, waiting in the open door: the specs, the jacket, the open-necked coloured shirt, the smile. Twelve years between first encounter and first meeting.

◆

Eddie took to the bibliography idea—as complete a survey of his work as could be made—with typical gusto.

Later, thinking over what this said about him, I concluded there were several things in play: vanity, no doubt, even in such a self-effacing chap; consciousness of his own worth; awareness of his legacy; comparison with other writers—and, knowing Eddie, possibly curiosity. Whatever the motivation, his enthusiasm for the project never dimmed.

He proved to be an orderly soul at heart (unlike myself), as I discovered in his study—the neatly arranged and labelled box files of correspondence, lectures, notes, etc—and over the next ten years he continued happily to discuss the recording of his work, the different categories into which it might be divided and into which to put the astonishing (to me) variety of stuff he produced.

His interest in categorising was often shared in his letters:

> The speech ... is to be printed in the university Gazette, so I suppose that will be one more item to record— under what?... *The Bridge* [1960] is actually the script of a film which was made by a scientist colleague of mine at the university [Crawford Robbie], and shown there; he was a great film enthusiast and ran the University Film Society. Does a film-script poem go in a separate category? Problems! Problems! [Letter, 22 May, 1981]

I had mentioned the lengths to which some fans and even biographers will go, even rummaging in their quarries' dustbins for communications or any scraps of interest. Eddie replied:

> Speaking of dustbins, I of course belong to the post-dustbin era, and all my rubbish is swept down a common chute to mingle with the ashes of 35 other houses, and who, as Sir Thomas Browne might say, will recompose into their separate individuations such a disjected and incoherent tohu-bohu and congeries of fragments? And then the great council remora comes and sucks it all away. [Ibid.]

Riffs such as this make his letters and postcards a joy to read.

In my new post at the library I was beginning to build up the collection of manuscripts by contemporary Scottish writers—numerous authors' papers seemed to end up in America. The American institutions were/are much more aggressive in their collecting: wining and dining potential donors, scanning obituaries, etc. I tentatively asked Eddie if there was anything he could let the Mitchell have. The result was that he had a kind of sixtieth birthday clear-out and the library acquired a wonderfully varied collection of original material: not only manuscripts (including his translation of *Beowulf* and early short stories), but drawings from his school days, surrealist table mats he had made in the 1930s, and his complete collection of photographic slides—perfect for exhibitions.

Work on the bibliography was continued mainly by correspondence. (Dear Hamish. Dear Eddie.) On 29 May 1981, he sent me a bunch of cuttings and offprints of poems dating from 1952 to 1979 'which you might as well have if they are of interest.' They were, as everything was. My plan included section A: Books by; and section C: Contributions to periodicals. He wrote:

> As regards the bibliography layout, I wonder whether the translations should be in a separate section (I mean books translated, which are in 'A' at the moment)? Or is it more usual to list all books together, whether original or translated? As regards the concrete/visual material, I'm not sure how far it would be possible to treat it separately—but I must think about this. I suppose ideally one would want the bibliography to be helpful to someone who wanted information about the concrete/visual side of my work. By the way, will 'C' include reviews? The number of reviews I've written over the years is horrible to contemplate! [Letter, 29 May 1981]

The answer to the last question was yes, and maybe at some time there would be a collection of the best of them—they made fascinating reading. Eddie made a point of reviewing genres he didn't specialise in himself: drama (for *Encore* and *The Times*—as the latter's 'Special Correspondent'—in the 1950s and 1960s) and fiction (for the *New Statesman* and *The Listener* in the 1960s and 1970s), although he had reviewed almost anything for *The Times Literary Supplement* over the previous thirty-five years. His output of literary journalism was prodigious.

The issue over translations took a while to resolve, but eventually translated poems were listed along with original poems—translating other authors' poems being almost as important to Eddie as writing his own. Back in the late 1940s and 1950s when he was in the doldrums with his own writing, he would channel his energy into translating.

Another evening visit followed, on 29 June 1981, as recorded in the bibliographical notebook I had begun to keep: 'V. pleasant ... mellow with Glenmorangie. Delicious crisps.' I asked Eddie if he had discovered (as I had) that the last line of his poem 'Strawberries' was missing from the recent paperback edition of *The Second Life*.

He said he'd found out the hard way—at a poetry reading. He read the poem and, although something told him there should be another line completing the poem ('we're so hypnotised by the printed word') he (and the book page) just stopped at 'hills'. He'd sent his dozen complimentary copies back to Edinburgh University Press and they'd returned them with the last line reinstated. Eddie wasn't sure how they had accomplished this, but on examination I was able to tell him that the leaf (pp.59–60) was a 'cancel' (that is, part of a book substituted for what was originally printed)—almost. It looked as though the leaf had been removed and the final line over-printed: the inking wasn't as black as the other lines.

I would have to check public copies to see if the correction had been made—all grist to the bibliographic mill. I went round the bookshops examining copies (a nuisance no doubt to the staff) and found they had indeed been changed.

I also asked him if he'd had anything published in the school magazine at Rutherglen Academy, before he went to the High School of Glasgow. The answer was yes, but he had no copies or details. The earliest published poem I was able to find was 'Song of the Flood', from the *High School of Glasgow Magazine*, April 1936. It was signed 'KAA', the youthful pseudonym which he used until 1939.

What do pseudonyms tell us about their adopters? Kaa is the rock python in Kipling's *Jungle Book*, one of the boy Mowgli's animal friends and mentors. As James McGonigal notes in his biography of Eddie, Kaa is an important pseudonym, 'a significant expression of his writing self.' Did Eddie see himself in Kipling's description of Kaa:

> [...] stretched out on a warm ledge in the afternoon sun, admiring his beautiful new coat, for he had been in retirement for the last ten days changing his skin, and now he was very splendid—darting his blunt-nosed head along the ground, and twisting the thirty

feet of his body into fantastic knots and curves, and
licking his lips as he thought of his dinner to come [...].
He turned twice or thrice in a big circle, weaving his
head from right to left. Then he began making loops
and figures of eight with his body, and soft, oozy tri-
angles that melted into squares and five-sided figures,
and coiled mounds, never resting, never hurrying,
and never stopping his low humming song.

['Kaa's Hunting', *Jungle Book* Chapter 3]

At a celebration of Eddie's sixty-fifth birthday at the Third Eye
Centre, he was presented with a cake with an image of Kaa iced
onto it, and I read the last sentence quoted above to him. 'Never
resting, never hurrying' seemed particularly appropriate. In
Kaa's last appearance in Kipling's stories ('Spring Running'),
he tells Mowgli, who is about to leave the jungle, 'it is hard to
cast the skin.' Were the seeds of a second life being sown here,
in the fledgling writer's mind? 'Ts! Ts!' said Kaa, weaving his
head to and fro. 'I have also known what love is. There are tales
I could tell that— '

Eddie also remembered that the first poem he wrote was
about nature (the details are now lost). He showed me where
he kept large posters—in the top section of his wardrobe. I
noticed Ian Hamilton Finlay's glass *waverock* on the window
ledge where the light could come through it (it's now in the
Scottish Poetry Library). We looked at the view. 'It's a great
place for birds, wood pigeons and magpies.' I asked if he had
written a magpie poem. No, he said.

But he was always alert to suggestion and later wrote about
this particular bird in 'A Defence', from his sequence *Hold
Hands Among the Atoms*, 1991. He then took me to his study
where there were eight or nine box files of cuttings and correspondence which I was welcome to look through. I would need
a day at least, I thought—little did I know. He lent me his own
list of published work to compare notes with till the next time
I came.

And one last thing I learned that evening was that Eddie
didn't alter or rewrite his poems after their first printing. At
least that reduced the need to go chasing after different versions for the bibliography! Eddie then went off to his summer

time-share at Kinloch Rannoch (Studio Lodge No. 8, Loch Rannoch Hotel) for his annual retreat (where his dream of a week's peace and quiet writing proved nebulous, as he told me later) and afterwards to Loughborough University to receive an honorary D. Litt. (sponsored by my former schoolmate Robin Hamilton, who lectured there and who was a long time fan). I continued to pursue enquiries on my own.

I was increasingly driven by the bibliographic hunt, and so was Eddie. After he returned from his break, I spent a whole day at Whittinghame Court on 5 August for what he called my 'big sift'. He wrote that I was to come early and 'just carry on as long as it takes. Sustenance of some sort will be provided'.

Which it was, in the form of a lunch nicely set out on a trolley in the sitting room: vegetable stew and strawberries and cream. 'Coffee passim,' I recorded.

I was of course suitably grateful for the hospitality and said so in a letter, thanking Eddie both for this and his endurance of the bibliographic 'third degree' (more pestering). I had completely lost track of time in the study among the papers and books. It seemed to me a whole lost literary under-jungle waiting for its explorer/archaeologist (i.e. me).

Some time after lunch, Eddie asked me about tea. I thought it was three o'clock. It was five-thirty. I had managed to look through only three out of ten boxes, spending too much time noting unpublished stuff—talks, lectures, etc—but not wanting to miss anything. The bibliography was well and truly underway. What I didn't realise until later was the extent of what Eddie was giving up in letting me stay so long. He was unable to write if someone else was in the flat. Even when he was with John Scott, the love of his life, they never lived together (except at weekends and on holidays). As I worked, I could hear Eddie pacing about the house every now and then. In my naivety it never occurred to me that he wasn't about his creative business. He probably did some admin, wrote letters, maybe a spot of reviewing—I hope I didn't waste his time too much.

19 August was another day with the box files. This time I started earlier—'Come at 9 a.m. rather than 10 next Wednesday if you want to have a longer session'—and I tried to work faster. Instead of copying all details I just made brief notes—

dates of periodical articles, for instance, to be checked out in the library later.

Lunch this time was Mexican rice and asparagus, a half bottle of white wine, biscuits and cheese and coffee. Over the meal Eddie showed me a pre-1914 Russian futurist anthology (which included his favourite Mayakovsky). We discussed the Russian use of *tirage* (print-run) as a publishing term for edition or impression. Apparently the Russians took a lot of similar terms from the French. Russian books give many more publishing details than British books: number of copies printed, names of editor, designer, art editor, for instance—very useful for a bibliographer. I finished Box 8 about 5.30.

Before I left, Eddie handed me the typescript of Alasdair Gray's novel *Lanark* (which the author had given him in return for Eddie's encouragement of its writing): it was a donation to the Mitchell Library and certainly a major coup for the manuscript collection.

I finally finished the boxes on 29 September. I also took a look at Eddie's Russian file and the files of his 'Preview' column, which he had written for *Radio Times* in the 1970s (in 1961 he had a column in the *Scottish Daily Express* as well—'Poetry in rock 'n roll sends me, says Edwin Morgan' was one heading).

I was given lunch again: stuffed peppers and potatoes (tinned), bread, a carafe of rosé, biscuits and Port Salud and Arran cheeses and coffee (Kenco coffee bags, he told me—'I've tried them all!'). He was working on a *Times Literary Supplement* review of the poet Eugenio Montale, whose work he had translated and who'd just died. I was finding the whole bibliographical process with Eddie hugely educative—it got me reading things (and poets) I hadn't encountered before. My horizons were expanding all the time.

Sifting through the boxes, I picked up all sorts of interesting titbits. For example, there was the 1964 letter from the literary editor of *The Glasgow Herald* saying they couldn't print Eddie's poem, 'An Addition to the Family', which was about the poet Maurice Lindsay acquiring a basset hound. It was was felt to be too much of a private joke between Eddie and Maurice. (It was published the following year, however, in the *Glasgow Review*). And I discovered that the cover of *The Second Life* was designed by the great book designer George Mackie.

And so it went on, the exchange of information, the questions and the answers, Eddie taking pleasure in worrying over the technicalities of bibliography-compiling as much as simply seeing a record of his work taking shape: 'Is it a publication or a "publication"?' he would ask; and 'I look forward to your next bout of speleology.'

With his encouragement, I began writing to publishers to see if they might be interested in publishing the bibliography. None of them was: no money in it and probably considered boring. Eddie thought Edinburgh University Press, who had published *The Second Life*, might be interested. In a letter that September, he said he thought they might 'enjoy the challenge of doing a good complex printing job, and of course the connection with my work is already there. In addition it would be pleasing to have it published in Scotland.'

I didn't actually write to EUP until April of the following year. Vivian Bone turned it down on behalf of the press: they were unable to offer publication since they weren't really doing much on the poetry front, but hoped I might find a small poetry publisher: 'best wishes with it anyway.'

When the bibliography was eventually published in 1990 (modified to 'Edwin Morgan: A Checklist') as Chapter Twelve of *About Edwin Morgan*, edited by Robert Crawford of St Andrews University and myself, and published by EUP, Vivian Bone laughingly accused me of getting it in 'by the back door'.

One thing from which I *couldn't* wean Eddie was his annoying (to me) habit of removing the dust jackets from books he'd bought and then discarding them, sometimes cutting bits from them and sticking them with sellotape on to the endpapers. He obstinately refused to accept (although I'm sure he did recognise) the value of dust jackets as bibliographical evidence, while knowing their presence added financial value to some books. He wasn't a 'collector'. He collected to read, and the jackets were a fussy irrelevance. I suspect he just thought they were untidy. His shelves may have been neat but they were rather drab to look at. This practice is possibly related to his long-time 'quite ruthless' (as he said) habit of cutting up pages of books and magazines for his series of scrapbooks.

Visits to Eddie's flat occasionally led to poems of my own. Inspired by the Anniesland gasometer visible from his kitchen window (immortalised later by Eddie himself in 'Gasometer' in *Cathures*, 2002), I wrote 'Gasometer Follies', imagining future cities building versions of such outworn edifices as 'crazy graces'. I sent him a copy.

He thanked me, praised some of the phrases ('a stac of rubble in a field of blaes') and gently wondered 'if the last two lines need some sharpening or tightening up?'

Which of course they did. With his response he enclosed a couple of souvenirs of his recent British Council visit to Israel (which included his main publisher, Michael Schmidt of Carcanet Press). One of these mementoes was his Masada cable car ticket which, he said, 'may be unimpressive, but the trip itself is spectacular.'

This set a pattern: I became the happy recipient of all sorts of Morgan ephemera—posters, fliers, invitations, name tags, tickets—an unofficial archivist, or at least a proxy hoarder! He was 'kicking the cumber / into others' vaults' as he later wrote in the poem 'To the Librarians', addressed to the Glasgow University Librarian Henry Heaney and myself about his papers and books vanishing into library maws. A note with one poster says:

> The enclosed, for your collection, is where I was last night. Jimmy Reid was in the same dressing-room. While waiting for his time to go on stage, he sat at a table eating a banana and writing an article on the Polish crisis, which he then had to phone through to a newspaper. There's something extremely engaging about him—Scotland's powerless Lech Walesa

Are there echoes here of the Polish acrobat Cinquevalli, whom Eddie much admired? (He was 'talking to some friends, / at the same time writing a letter with one hand / and with the other juggling four balls'—from 'Cinquevalli', Eddie's own favourite of all his poems, published the previous year).

On 8 May 1982, Eddie sent me a postcard saying he had enjoyed a display at the Mitchell Library of contemporary Scottish manuscripts which I had organised: 'Keep collecting!' The display was in the foyer of the recently opened extension and included manuscripts from an important donation by Glasgow poet Tom Buchan, as well as a screen showing a looped selection from the huge number of transparencies acquired from Eddie in 1980, under the title 'Edwin Morgan Slides'.

I sent him a revised layout of the bibliography before I went on holiday to the Isle of Arran. There I received a letter:

> Thanks for the latest bibliographical arrangement, which I shall brood over. Where would the STV film about me, or the 7 Poets video, fit in? Don't answer that: you're on holiday!

Was Eddie becoming as obsessive as I was?

But being on holiday didn't stop the biblio-mill grinding. I decided to produce my own Edwin Morgan publication to add to the 'A' section. With my Imperial 200 portable manual typewriter (which I always took on holiday), paper, scissors and stapler, I printed and bound three copies of an edition of Eddie's nine one-word poems. These had appeared in No. 25 of Ian Hamilton Finlay's magazine *Poor.Old.Tired.Horse.* (November 1967), but had never been collected in book form (and weren't, properly, until *Dreams and Other Nightmares*, 2010). I gave it the imprint 'Mariscat Press', named after the street where we lived in Pollokshields on Glasgow's south side, and sent the first two copies of the tiny booklet to Eddie on 20 May.

In his letter of thanks a few days later, he described it as his 'parvum opus' and expressed a hope that it would be the first production of many:

> Will you do more copies of the one-words—distribute them?—sell them?—or stop at three? [I stopped at three.] Actually Mariscat would be a fine mysterious name for a small private press.

I replied that I liked the name—and so the Mariscat Press was born, not as a private press (we never printed our books ourselves, although we did have a few items printed letterpress for us as limited editions) but as the proverbial small press.

In July I sent him a copy of the first proper Mariscat publication, *XII from Catullus*, translations from the Latin into Glaswegian by David Neilson. He replied, 'Vivat Mariscat.'

I had teamed up with my friend Kevin McCarra in this new venture and we were soon publishing Eddie himself: firstly a hand-printed card of his poem 'Grendel', then the following year a real book, *Grafts/Takes*. We were gradually becoming his de facto Scottish publisher, bringing out pamphlets and books in between his main collections from Carcanet, continuing until the last book before his death, the previously mentioned *Dreams and Other Nightmares*. As Eddie and I became more comfortable with each other, this professional relationship slipped into a friendship. He began reciprocal visits to my family flat in Pollokshields—a Glasgow West-Ender venturing into darkest south side!

◆

As mentioned earlier, I had tracked down the poems and stories Eddie had published in the *High School of Glasgow Magazine*, but had never managed to get hold of any copies of the school magazine of Rutherglen Academy (now Stonelaw High School) which Eddie attended (and hated) from 1928 to 1934. However, in a letter (17 September 1982) he sent me the text of one he had remembered ('at least I think I have') which was in French—and here it is:

Oui monsieur,
C'est le café—
Noir comme le diable
Et chaud comme l'enfer.

He commented:

The fact that I thought 'café' rhymes with 'enfer' shows the poem comes from my first year of learning French!

That first year would probably have been 1932/33, making this his earliest recorded poem. He continued:

Being determined to keep you busy, I have just finished a new sequence of 26 poems called AN ALPHA-BET OF GODDESSES.

And keep me busy he did, until the bibliography was published in 1990—and later too. After the first flurry of bibliographical enthusiasm from 1980 to 1982, things settled down to a more regular routine of collecting material and exchanging information. Eddie may have retired from the English Department of Glasgow University in 1980, but there was no retiring from things literary—he threw himself into the life freelance: the number of readings and talks, the number of commissions, the amount of writing time, all increased, with the consequent increase of appearances in print—and indeed of ephemera flying around—all requiring to be recorded. The arrangement of the bibliography (or checklist, as it was now properly called) was more or less agreed, as follows, for those interested:

A Books, etc by, translated by or edited by EM
B Books containing contributions by or co-edited by EM
C Contributions to periodicals and press
D Interviews
E Ephemera
F Odds and Ends
G Manuscripts
H Recordings
I Musical Settings
J Critical and biographical works and articles about EM

Publication of the checklist in 1990 (which came to over one hundred pages) did not, of course, mean the end of bibliographing. I continued to collect and note material over the years, with Eddie's help as ever. (By now—Love, Eddie. Love, Hamish.) There was always the intention of bringing out a supplement and it's a major regret that it never happened before he died.

At the time of writing, I've listed most material published between 1989 and 2010 (and later) with some items previously missed. Discussion continues with various bodies about putting it online (with the original checklist). Since 2004, when I moved to Edinburgh, almost all of my Edwin Morgan collection has been housed in the Scottish Poetry Library. It is splendidly organised and catalogued as their 'Edwin Morgan Archive'. There was a grand opening of the Archive on Eddie's eighty-ninth birthday in 2009. As recorded in Jim McGonigal's biography, *Beyond the Last Dragon* (2012), Eddie thought the collection should have stayed in Glasgow (where he thought the Scottish Poetry Library should have been as well—he was incredibly Glasgow-centric) and was not keen to attend. It was only after Jim had bought him a T-shirt, showing a Tunnock's

Caramel Wafer over the slogan 'Glasgow Takes the Biscuit', to wear under his jacket, that he agreed to go. And made sure everyone noticed the T-shirt!

But he did actually enjoy the occasion. There were nice speeches from Mike Russell (Culture Minister) and Eddie's old friend Ron Butlin (Edinburgh's Makar). I said a few words to the effect that I was pleased that what was once mine was now available to everybody. Eddie was transported in his wheelchair by lift to the basement to see where the Archive was housed and where his desk, chair and typewriter had been placed.

More recent material is now also in the Scottish Poetry Library, as an addition to the Archive. I hope it will be useful to those who, as I said in the introduction to the 1990 checklist, are determined to pursue Eddie's whittrick (weasel or stoat) to its many and various bolt-holes. As Iain Sinclair put it in a review of a book about David Gascoyne, 'bibliography offers as powerful a storyline as biography' (*Guardian Review*, 31 March 2012). For me, bibliography offered a friendship that had a major impact on my life.

To finish this section, here are a few examples showing how Eddie kept a self-interested eye on the ever-expanding list of Morganiana—sometimes giving a little nudge to the storyline. In 1984, I was checking out his contributions to the *Glasgow University Magazine* (GUM) and came across a poem 'To Sandra' in the issue of 3 May 1939. I must have asked him, 'Who is Sandra? What is she?'

'You're digging me up!' he complained, but good-humouredly. The poem begins 'I am that city, granite of your tears' and is in fact a riposte to an earlier poem in GUM, 'This Sombre Evening' by 'Sandra', which begins, 'Over the city pallid night is drawn'.

Eddie often liked to be mischievously mysterious, as in his continued refusal to identify the location of 'In the Snack-bar'. In 1990 he sent me a copy of a poem about his visit to Charterhouse School written by one of the housemasters, 'For your entertainment, if not for the bibliography', and on 6 December that same year he wrote:

Did you know that TAG Theatre Company are going to choreograph me (well, my work)? Do you have a bibliographical category for 'Poems Danced'? Nonny no, probably.

À propos of this, after the performance the following year, he sent me a review which referred to his poem 'Memories of Earth' as 'Memories of Edith'. 'A hitherto suppressed chapter—?' he pseudo-tantalised. He loved this kind of misprint (but had a hawk's eye for them in his own published work)—such as the gender-changing reference, that every now and then cropped up, 'Edwina' Morgan.

Things came full circle a few years ago, when the scholar Greg Thomas, in quest of material for an article on the Scottish Poetry Library's Edwin Morgan Archive, visited me and I let him look through the box files of my Morgan correspondence—while I prowled or pottered through the house looking for things to do. I made sure he had a mug of coffee and a plate of chocolate digestive biscuits, the least I could offer. I hope Eddie would have approved the turn—and the sustenance.

In revisiting the checklist I've been surprised by things I had forgotten, and by how many items were *not* included in the published listing (probably for reasons of space). And looking through the letters, postcards (we both had a postcard mania), notes, ephemera and all the rest, I realise that I didn't know what an extraordinary treasure was being built up—someone gradually unfolding his life to you bit by bit of paper. It is a wonderful legacy of a literary life and an unforgettable friendship.

3. Alone

Eddie has often been described as reclusive or private. He was, and he wasn't. He enjoyed company and conversation (especially one to one), but he wasn't a pubby poet or much of a drinker, even. Many writers have told of reading with him at some event, then Eddie not always having a drink with them afterwards but slipping off for the second last train home. I understand this. I play in a band and often feel similarly—the gig is the thing. I go to play, enjoy playing with other musicians, but then I want to go home. What he certainly did like was a lunch in company—see the section on lunches. He wasn't, for example, one of the Edinburgh Milne's Bar crowd —MacCaig, MacDiarmid et al.

Alexander Moffat's *Seven Poets* painting portrays Eddie about right, sitting by himself apart—in, but not of, the other poets' world. If he was in a pub in Glasgow, it would probably be with a male date (as I have seen). I remember him telling me that when the owners of Milne's Bar wanted to redecorate the pub in the style it had been in the 1950s when it was frequented by the poets (even painting the walls and ceiling nicotine brown), they asked Eddie if he would write a poem for the occasion. He refused. He wasn't part of that scene, he said.

He was an only child and used to being on his own. He enjoyed the camaraderie (and sexual encounters) of the army during the war, but is on record as saying he couldn't settle to write then. Later on, in 1962, when he moved out of his parents' house into his own flat, he embraced the freedom to be alone, to suit himself. He set his course early in life—work was the purpose, working with literature, and he worked best on his own.

Writers vary in this regard. I share a house with my partner, the poet and children's writer Diana Hendry, but we have different writing habits. Diana, like Eddie, can't write properly when someone else is in the house. She prefers quiet, and can sit at her desk for hours on end; whereas I like music on (mainly Radio 3), can't sit at a desk for long, am restless and have ideas when I least expect them. So I have a separate writing place and actually go out to work each morning. Eddie, as I said, couldn't share a house for any length of time. I still feel guilty at all the days I spent at his flat, going through his papers and books while he was there in the background, but am grateful for his sacrifice.

He did enjoy visitors—but always arranged beforehand. It's difficult to know the range and number of callers because, like many of us, Eddie compartmentalised his life, and didn't often talk to one friend about visits from another. One found out from the visitors themselves.

For instance, Ron Butlin has written of the visits by the 'Edinburgh Boys' (namely himself, Iain Banks, Andrew Greig, Ian Rankin, Ken MacLeod) to Whittinghame Court for grub and wine and chat, and latterly absinthe, as in his poem, 'Absinthe with Eddie'.

I myself had a couple of absinthe-with-Eddie sessions, the first of which was very enjoyable—especially the pleasure of watching the delight Eddie took in the rituals of absinthe, the pouring it over a sugar cube, for example. But the second was not so good: possibly I drank it too quickly or took too much—whatever, I was extremely ill afterwards.

4. Family Visits

Many literary friendships begin with correspondence—from fan letters to requests for permission to reprint. My first approach to Eddie was born of both. First, letters; then visits to Eddie's flat. In time we grew comfortable with each other and responded to each other's enthusiasms.

In 1982, two years after I had met Eddie, Winifred and I invited him to our flat in Mariscat Road for a meal. That was on 7 January, when our son Kenny was four years old and baby Christina nine months. And so he was introduced to our family. He reciprocated the following year, and gradually a pattern was established, of us going to Eddie's at New Year and him coming to us on or around his birthday in April, with other visits in between.

There were occasional outings too. For instance, in 1990 during Glasgow's reign as City of Culture, the Bolshoi Opera came to give a rare performance of Rimsky-Korsakov's opera-ballet, *Mlada*. As a Russophile Eddie was eager to see it and treated Winifred, myself and his friend Morven to tickets—at £75 each! Tickets sold slowly and the week before the event they were offered at £10 each. Eddie was not best pleased, and even less pleased to discover our expensive seats were so far back in the hanger-like space of the Exhibition Centre that we could hardly see what was happening on stage. I tried to mitigate things by buying us all strawberries and cream at the interval. (Eddie could be acerbic about opera. I accompanied him twice to Scottish Opera productions—one was 'too static' and the other 'had no tunes'.)

After I had brokered a deal between Eddie and Glasgow Libraries for the Mitchell Library to accept Eddie's library as a bequest, he thought of a great way to thin his book collection (there must have been at least 10,000 in his flat) and asked if he could donate volumes in advance of his death. Our annual visit to Eddie's thereafter always included loading up our car with bags of books accumulated in his spare room during the previous year. I would take them in to the Mitchell and catalogue them.

These were afternoon visits, usually on the Sunday after New Year's Day. The first time must have been a bit of an adventure for the children, not least crowding into the lift to Eddie's third-floor flat—the novel idea of going up in a lift to visit someone! He was always at the open door to welcome us, dressed in his usual smart casual way, jacket and open-necked shirt. He went to town on hospitality, setting out a huge array of goodies: biscuits, sweets, nibbles and several kinds of drink. And he always had interesting toys and puzzles for the children. Eddie became a kind of adopted uncle to our children, a relationship that continued into their adulthoods.

Kenny and Christina still recall these early outings. Christina remembers all the books that lined the walls of the flat (though she was used to that at home) and the way that annual visits to Eddie concluded with

> work to be done too—loading up the car with parcels
> of books neatly wrapped in brown paper. I seem to
> remember coming out in a rash from lifting these—
> maybe it was the dust.

She somehow knew that there was 'something special' about Eddie's place, with the books and artworks; and there was always a different 'futuristic' gadget each time. For example, there was a 'clever' paperweight, and the spaceman's pen we gave Eddie as a present (it could write upside down in zero gravity—just right, we thought, for him). She also recalls watching a video of fish, whales, sharks, etc on his television. 'Very soothing,' he told her. And he laid out the sweets, fruit jellies, etc in lots of lovely plates and bowls. Christina now has one of these bowls in the hall of her Dublin flat. Other things about Eddie have stayed in her mind too: the letters and cards he sent her, the cards usually depicting cats in some shape or other—she had one of a green cat hanging in her room for years. She loved his handwriting: 'so artistic and distinctive'.

Pride of place perhaps goes to the postcard she received from Santa Claus just before Christmas 1985 (when she was four), postmarked Rovaniemi (in the Arctic Circle). Oddly, the writing bears a close resemblance to Eddie's. (He blew the prize money from winning the Soros Award for translation on a day trip on Concorde to the North Pole to meet Santa Claus.) Kenny remembers that postcard too. 'That just seemed unreal to me. Santa Claus! And he *went* there!'

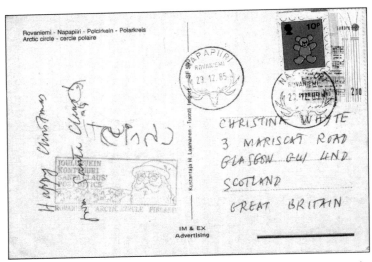

When Christina went off to London in 2001 to study music at Trinity College in Greenwich, Eddie gave her financial help (without my knowing) as well as 'wise words and good wishes'. I remember Eddie telling me that when he'd first heard a very young Christina play the piano, he felt 'here was something non-tentative'. (He was a good talent spotter.) 'Glad to hear Christina was safely stowed,' he wrote after I'd told him about the overnight journey to London (in a car driven by my old friend Leslie Verth) to deliver her to her hall of residence. We left her sitting on her bed weeping. Leslie and I stopped at Stratford on our way home for dinner and Shakespeare. On a walk along the bank of the Avon I phoned her to see how she was. I couldn't hear her very well. 'What's that noise?' I asked. 'Oh, I'm in the pub,' she said.

Strangely, Christina has a notion that Eddie had smoked at our house, perhaps at a writers' party. Eddie, of course, was a non-smoker (though he smoked in the army during the war, as they all did) but he famously loved the smell of cigarettes ('One Cigarette', etc) and kept a box of them on the table in his sitting room. She's perhaps remembering (as I do) Eddie's friend Malcolm in our hall at one of our parties, rolling his own, and talking about it being something to occupy his hands (as many smokers feel). She has clear memories, as well, of visiting Eddie with me later in both his care homes. She wishes now she'd had the confidence and knowledge to have chatted more to him.

My son Kenny, too, loved the annual new year visits and felt it was a great way to end the festivities and a fun start to the new year. To him, Eddie was just another one of my friends, at least at first. It was years before he realised Eddie's talent and reputation—in fact, he says 'it was quite mind-blowing' when he did. He remembers Eddie as always kind and genuinely interested in him and what he was doing—not just politeness. And the visits were exciting because Eddie usually gave him a new puzzle. Kenny adored the puzzles. Maybe they were just to keep him occupied but Eddie was equally intrigued and attracted to some of them. With others, he didn't have a clue. Most of these puzzles are long gone but the best one, Kenny told me, he still has and he still hasn't solved it. It's a plastic figure of eight with balls in four colours—you have to move them around to join the colours together. He picks it up every month or so and has another go at it:

> I feel like I'll keep trying until I solve it for him, but I've no idea if I ever will. The furthest I've ever got is two colours properly done, but it's close just now— almost there ...

To Kenny, Eddie was pretty cool: he had a 'magic' clock on his mantelpiece (an atomic one) and the *Star Wars* videos, as well as lots of foreign films that looked interesting (he's sure Eddie introduced him to some, including Tarkovsky):

> There were so many other random objects to look at in his flat, plus the view was amazing. It was always fun going just for that. At the time I don't think I'd been in a block of flats, so the fact that it felt vaguely futuristic and strange just added to the attraction. I also think I loved it because it was similar to our flat in that there were wall-to-wall books—and a typewriter—but he had a balcony as well!

Nor has he forgotten Eddie visiting us in Pollokshields from time to time and how keen he would be to find out what Kenny was up to:

He was also always enthusiastic about my artistic attempts—he was positive about my photography, for one thing. Being asked for one of my photos for his book cover was an honour, needless to say.

The passion for photography lasted. Kenny (aged 22) was official photographer for Eddie's big eightieth birthday bash at the Kibble Palace in 2000. He was 'slightly amused at how sort of humble [Eddie] was, when it was clear he was so well respected and admired.' Kenny and I attended the first night of Eddie's play about Jesus (*A.D.*) at the Tramway in Glasgow on 20 September 2000. As Kenny arrived at the venue he was greeted with shouts of 'Judas!' from Pastor Jack Glass and his cohort of fundamentalists. While he and I were chatting before the performance with Alison Grey of Amnesty International, Glass threw thirty five-pence coins into the foyer. We picked them up and put them in Alison's collecting can.

Kenny saw Eddie less frequently once he was in the care home and getting frailer. 'But he was still Eddie. Even the last time I saw him, I remember him being pretty sharp. He had a beard too, which made him cooler!'

Eddie's 1988 Christmas card to the whole family was a large card with a cat on the front ('Meowy-y Christmas!') and a hand-written poem inside:

> May all you jolly southside cats
> Have furry paws and party hats
> And juicy plate of hot mince-pies
> And jimjam jellies cut to size
> And soups of greenies in the bowl
> To warm the cockles of the soul.
> All pussy bellies that be tim   [*empty*]
> Shall swell with goodies to the brim
> And make your toes turn out and in
> (The rhyming's getting slightly dim,
> So farewell all you cherubim!)

5. Children

As I have pointed out already, Eddie was an only child. He's on record as saying he would have liked a sibling. I have a brother myself, three and a half years younger, whom I love dearly. But (according to family history) when he was born and brought home, I took to my bed, and, as far as I remember for most of my childhood (to my shame) I more or less ignored him. I suppose I felt (or preferred to feel) like an only child—and I wonder if many firstborns feel like this or, probably more accurately, are temperamentally loners. After I began writing poems, at about the age of thirteen or fourteen, I spent a lot of my spare time closeted alone in the room I shared with Graeme, scribbling poems and stories and reading the dictionary. Our relations were better in later teens.

I wonder if Eddie would still have been a loner, even with a brother or sister. He did play with other children round his home in Burnside (as I did in Clarkston), but the only anecdote reported is of his playing in goal for the local street league. He told me he would have liked to have children of his own. He was fond of all young people. However, he was able to have proxy relatives of a sort. For example, he was part of his old friend Morven Cameron's family Christmas celebrations every year (there were lots of nephews and nieces), and he also attended her annual street garden party. And of course he was part of my own extended family, as I've said, enjoying our New Year visits and visiting us at Mariscat Road.

In 'A letter to Baron Munchausen', written as the introduction to his 'poetic reconstructions', *Tales from Baron Munchausen* (Mariscat, 2005), Eddie invented a son: he says that 'the full potential of narrative' struck him only after his encounter with 'the enchanting Leila', whom he met in Cairo during his war service. They kept in touch after the war and he was pleased when she wrote to tell him

> that our son Mahmoud had decided to study folklore and archaeology at the university, concentrating on the art of storytelling in Ancient Egypt. He eventually obtained a post in the Cairo Museum. As I look back now, I realise that he himself will soon be due for

retirement, which will leave him more time to be with his family and to fascinate his new grandson with stories his mother told him so long ago.

The press got hold of this and printed the story as news, apparently not realising it was in a book by a notorious teller of tall tales. They didn't get the 'joke', if it was a joke. It's interesting that the story featured a non-existent family and a son enjoying the role of narrator. It's wistful, revealing and touching. And actually just about within the bounds of possibility. Eddie *did* have a sexual encounter with 'Leila' in a Cairo bordello during the war, he told me, his only such encounter with a woman. So who knows?

In an interview with Robert Crawford in 1988, Eddie said:

I think that if I was married and was wanting to have a family, I'd want to have more than one child.

In *About Edwin Morgan* (1990) the writer Kevin McCarra commented on that statement:

If that reflection contains a sense of regret about his own youth, the reader, selfish as always, can scarcely wish that Morgan's life had been different.

6. History

A subtitle here might be: 'In which Eddie changed my perspective on history'.

My father loved history, his favourite subject at school, and I did too. I still have the four volumes of Churchill's *History of the English-Speaking Peoples* that my mother gave him, book by book as they were published. I remember childhood weekend excursions to Stirling Castle, Holyrood Palace, the Wallace Monument and other places of Scottish historical interest. I loved old buildings and once took home a stone filched from the Covenanters' watchtower near Dunoon and kept it for years, with a naive belief in its importance. My Primary Seven class at Carolside School was divided into four 'houses'. I was in Wallace and I was given the task of producing an end of term magazine for my house. I called it *Wallace Times* and it was my first taste of editing. I gathered the contents, wrote a story about William Wallace titled 'In Wallace Times' (which I thought very clever) and drew a broch for the cover illustration (with help from my mother). Little did I know ....

I studied history both at secondary school (writing essays influenced by Carlyle's style in his *French Revolution*) and university. Basically, I was fascinated by the past and struggled to comprehend what it was like for people to live then. I read historical fiction (Duggan, Treece, Warner, Sutcliff) and became addicted to historical films (from sword and sandal to documentary reconstruction).

I wasn't totally mired in the past, however. In my teens I subscribed (or at least my father did for me, and I had to give up *Melody Maker*) to *New Society*, admired the Swedish way of life, and had thoughts of becoming a sociologist or a prison reformer (to my teacher's surprise I chose a biography of Elizabeth Fry as a prize in an essay competition at school). A hopeless idealist. What I probably *didn't* do was connect poetry with any of it.

I married, had children, had a dream job working on old manuscripts in the local history department of Europe's largest reference library. Then I entered the world or worlds of Edwin Morgan. Reading his work, recording his work, talking with him, becoming a friend—I had to face up to the challenge of all this. His poems had obviously appealed to me: the imagination, the love poetry, the writing about my own city. But I had to grapple with outlook, not just description. Here was a relentless optimist, a believer in human progress regardless, convinced that poetry had to acknowledge science and the contemporary world and that what is important is now—and the future—not looking back. His motto was Change Rules OK (*Essays*, 1974). In *Nothing Not Giving Messages* (1991), he said:

> So much of my work has been about something that is in the process of change [...]. I'm more interested in what does change than in what has been and what is constant.

So he made me think, *re*think. It's a powerful thing when you meet someone who challenges your way of thought, your out-look—and, for a poet, your way of writing about it all. I believe it was good for me. I tried to 'acknowledge the present', to see the good in developing technology, to look to the future and not to be stuck in the past.

Except—there were contradictions. It wasn't that Eddie was not interested in history—on the contrary, he wrote about it constantly—but it wasn't history-text history; it was the nitty gritty of life and lives past, their nooks and crannies, looking at history aslant (see *Sonnets from Scotland* and *Planet Wave*). He liked to view the past not from the perspective of the present but imaginatively, from the perspective of the future. Hence the science fiction poems. I myself was never a great fan of sci-ence fiction (apart from Ray Bradbury and SF films)—crime fiction is more my thing. But I had to think about it. It was a way of seeing the past—and the present—more clearly. What Eddie *didn't* like (and here we agreed) was 'heritage', that fake worship of tradition, a sanitised and romanticised version of history.

There was also Eddie's passion for colour, especially colour photography—which might seem odd considering he was red/green colour blind. But maybe not—he still saw in colour, just different colours. This was another adjustment I had to make, given my personal preference for black and white photographs (Cartier-Bresson my hero) and films. The photographer Sally Soames claimed that black and white photography possessed 'a greater visual impact than colour' ('Sally Soames Obituary',

The Guardian, 26 October 2019). I suspect Eddie felt it falsified things, dramatised them, and that colour was more true, more real, certainly more modern.

He wasn't very good with electrical appliances, as I discovered. I can still see him on his sitting room floor frustratedly fiddling with the video recorder and television. Of course, there's no reason why a science fiction writer has to be able to connect cables, but in his poems Eddie was considered *the* poet of technology.

Yet he never took to, or used, a computer. He was persuaded to buy an Amstrad when they came out (November 1985) but it sat in pieces on the desk in his study for weeks, unlooked at and unloved, till he finally gave it away to a friend. He stuck to his manual typewriter all his working life—the famous Adler Blue Bird—and couldn't be persuaded even to try an electric one. Eddie, the steampunk poet?

As I've got older, I've become more of an optimist. I still think the universe is meaningless in general, but we just have to do what we can to lessen the meaninglessness. And I believe with Eddie that 'nothing is not giving messages', that everyone and everything has a story to tell or be told. There's a phrase of Wordsworth's, 'things speaking forever', that might be said to anticipate this dictum. And I've become a fan of the Radio Four programme, *The Life Scientific*—I love the enthusiasm of the scientists who talk to Jim Al-Khalili. Enthusiasm is the key.

I confess that after Eddie died I felt a little bit of relief. Not at his death, of course. Just that I no longer needed to keep up— not a pretence really—but more a constant acknowledgement of present and future (why did I feel this?). There was relief that I could maybe, now and then, slump into the past. I've recently been writing a sequence of poems about my childhood in the suburbs, without worrying whether Eddie would approve—he rarely wrote about his childhood, and this was deliberate.

But I suppose we all want approval of some sort for what we do. I love jazz—most forms of it—while Eddie, despite working with the jazz musician Tommy Smith on several works, wasn't keen on this type of music . He once called it 'old men in suits', as if a man in a suit and tie couldn't swing or improvise. Perhaps it was the improvisation he didn't take to. One thing we *did* share was what might be called a middle-class left-wing nationalism—and a vision of a future Scottish socialist republic. Neither of us was ever a member of the Scottish National Party but we usually voted for it.

7. Nineteen Kinds of Barley

In July 1984 my family and I took a new house for our annual summer holiday on the Isle of Arran. This was Myrtlebank Cottage, Bungalow Road, at the north end of Lamlash. We rented it from Irene and Sandy, of the well-known local Sillars family (which includes the novelist John Sillars). We'd rented from the family in the past and had got to know them quite well. For the next fifteen years we returned annually to this cottage.

Opposite the bungalows was a large field, usually kept empty. However, this year it was being used for a 'Barley Variety Demonstration'. With rows of white markers for the different varieties, it looked more like a war cemetery.

I was fascinated by the names of the barley varieties and listed them in my diary: Javelin, Natasha, Acclaim, Doublet, Nairn, Corgi, Piccolo, Kym, Lina, Vista, Delta, Themis, Flare, Klaxon, Gold Marker, Golf, Celt, Golden Promise, Midas. Thinking Eddie might be interested, I sent the list to him.

A vintage postcard showing a field of barley being harvested (an advert for Glen Spey Pure Malt Whisky) soon arrived. Dated 24 July, it read;

> You will be pleased to know that the samples of barley
> you dispatched from Arran have been planted and a
> crop is confidently expected. More in due course.

Eddie always seemed to have an appropriate postcard for any occasion. Nor could he ever write a boring one. Another card later that month hoped we were 'all enjoying the myrtle banks, bungalows, lambs, lunches, eels, rams, etc.'

In early August, the 'crop' was duly delivered, a typed copy of 'Nineteen Kinds of Barley' in a letter dated 31 July, the poem signed with Eddie's monogram.

He had rearranged alphabetically the names I had sent. It was a splendid list poem, the sort of thing Eddie did so well, perfectly illustrating what W. N. Herbert later called 'his sense of the magical life of the list'. In *About Edwin Morgan* (1990), Herbert went on to describe the poem as 'celebratory with a kind of epic tone, playing on the gap between an individual strain's characteristics and the associative strands it has for a layperson'. In due course, 'Nineteen Kinds of Barley' saw publication in the first issue of the new Scottish poetry magazine

Verse (October 1984), and it was included in Eddie's next Carcanet collection, *Themes on a Variation* (1988).

Obviously flushed with onlie-begetterism, I tried again the following summer, sending a list of Arran potato varieties grown in the grounds of the Heritage Museum in Brodick: Pilot, Comrade, Peak, Rose, Consul, Banner, Signet, Viking, Comet, Chief, Crest, Victory. Eddie sent the result on 21 July 1985:

> Thanks for the list of varieties, but your potato-growers lack the imagination of the barley-folk, and the following is the best I can do (it's not much):
>
> CONSUL is not quite the clean one.
>
> SIGNET is a hot one.
>
> PILOT is all eyes.
>
> ROSE is a croquette.
>
> VIKING is a masher.
>
> PEAK is pure granite chips.
>
> COMRADE is in his old jacket.
>
> VICTORY is piping skirlie.
>
> BANNER is a patch.
>
> COMET is a trail of peelings.
>
> CREST is crisp.
>
> CHIEF is Raleigh the Reiver.
>
> I doubt if that will please the Arran Potato Marketing Board, unless on the principle that all advertising is good advertising.... I hope you are all determinedly enjoying yourselves, hanging up oilskins, shaking umbrellas, watching watergaws, etc.

That tells us what the weather was like at least. Eddie kindly let me include the piece in *The Glasgow Magazine* (1985) and later in my *Arran Anthology* (1997), but it is otherwise quietly buried. From then on I concentrated on publishing Eddie's poems rather than trying to inspire them.

G12 0BG - 24 -7-1984

You will be pleased to know
that the samples of
barley you dispatched
from Arran have
been planted and
a crop is confidently
expected. More
in due course.

Regards,

POST CARD

THIS ADDRESS TO BE WRITTEN ON THIS SPACE ONLY

HAMISH WHYTE

3. MARISCAT ROAD

GLASGOW G41 4ND

GREENWICH
1884 / MERIDIAN - 1984
16P

8 Cut the Last Line

Eddie was well-known never to refuse a request for advice about writing when asked. He was a great encourager, especially of younger writers. He helped Alasdair Gray during the long gestation of *Lanark*, as mentioned earlier, as well as countless other would-be authors. I know he also gave tactful advice to one of my friends about a novel he was writing (the novel never materialised).

I recently met the writer Des Dillon at the Nairn Festival. Over coffee Des told me that he had once been at a reading with Eddie; and afterwards 'kidnapped' him and quizzed him for some writing advice. 'Write the way you speak,' Eddie told him. And, said Des, that's what he did—and still does—to great effect, as we heard that morning in Nairn.

When I first met Eddie, I was thirty-two and had been writing poems for about eighteen years. I'd had one pamphlet published (by John Bishop's Autolycus Press) and some poems in magazines and newspapers.

My early poetry path had been formed mainly through school reading: Coleridge ('The Rime of the Ancient Mariner'), Wordsworth ('Michael'), Browning ('My Last Duchess' and everything else, even 'Mr Sludge the Medium'), Dryden ('Alexander's Feast'), Shakespeare (especially *Macbeth*); third year discovery of Auden and Lawrence; then, discovered for myself, Plath, Cummings and Sir Gawain.

My late teens and early twenties were ruled by David Jones and Robert Graves. I remember a university friend telling me *The White Goddess* (which I carried about like a bible) was a dangerous book. But by 1980 I had emerged from the thrall of the *Goddess*, and Cummings (whom Graves championed) had led me to Carlos Williams and Reznikoff and Oppen. And of course there was Eddie and discovering through him that you could write about anything, even a brief scene seen from a bus (I still think 'Linoleum Chocolate' is a key poem). Not to mention the other Glasgow poets such as Liz Lochhead and Tom Leonard.

When I started writing poems, I showed them to my family and got little encouragement, despite my mother being a poetry lover (maybe that's why). They were terrible, but that wasn't the point. From then on, I tended to shut myself away to write in the bedroom I shared with my brother. At one point I could have been found, for example, working on an epic (in the stanza form of *Sir Gawain and the Green Knight*) about the white knight who makes a brief appearance in Arthurian legend, while listening to the radio (where I heard Sylvia Plath's last broadcast and whose voice has echoed in my head ever since). And I had never showed my poems again to anyone except, later on, the girls I wrote verses to (and even then, not always) and, later still, poet friends. I never asked advice, which of course I regret now. I was probably afraid, as many are, of criticism.

And so when I met Eddie, got to know him and his work, recorded his publications, I somehow didn't feel at first that I could show him my own writing. I had the vague notion it would have been exploitative—a kind of inverted snobbery, no doubt.

And anyway, wasn't I already being exploitative enough? Visiting his home, pestering him with questions, rummaging through his books and papers—as bad as a demented fan raking through his hero's dustbins!

But at least it was a two-way process. Eddie got an in-house archivist and recorder of his work, and later, also a publisher.

Eventually I did show him some of my own poems. The first would have been 'Gasometer Follies' (mentioned earlier), inspired by the view from his kitchen window of the dark looming shape of the Anniesland gasometer. And, looking through my correspondence with Eddie, I was surprised to find I'd shared more with him than I'd thought. It must have seemed too good an opportunity to pass up.

For example, I sent him two poems in 1987, one called 'Calendaring', a forty-line piece I'd written for Winifred's fortieth birthday—based on my work at the Mitchell Library cataloguing eighteenth-century family papers—and another, 'Guiser', about a fox I'd seen on Hallowe'en.

On the topic of the poems and significant birthdays, Eddie wrote:

> Thanks very much for the two poems, both of which I
> really like—especially the gulravage [a word I'd taken

from an old letter], the claret, the sand, and the green man. You must certainly get these in print. ['Guiser', yes, I did.] 40's all right actually; enjoy, as they say. 80's not so good unless you're Olivier. 120's probably not advisable unless you live in the Caucasus and have an ample supply of yogurt.

Two years later I must have shown him my collection of Arran poems, *Siva in Lamlash*, because he wrote:

Siva is an attractive gathering and I hope it really does appear! Machrie—yes, well, I remember a peril of bulls in Glen Sannox. Nice to see Bungalow Road returning to its origins.

Stephen Gill of Whiting Bay was to have published the *Siva* poems under his Arran Gallery imprint, but he was so dilatory I gave up. Gael Turnbull eventually brought it out as one of his 'minimal missive' series in 1991.

In 1990, the poet James Fenton ran a competition in *The Observer* for an 'emergent poem' in the style of Eddie's 'Message Clear' (and others). I entered a piece that concluded with Emily Dickinson's line 'There is no frigate like a book'. I was not successful.

'I'm sorry your frigate didn't make the winning gun,' wrote Eddie. 'I still like it for all that'.

And in 1991, of my 'Playground Fires', he wrote: 'I like the playground poem which contains something very precisely.'

He was a constant friend, and constantly encouraging.

For many years I've been working on translations of Books XIII and XIV of the Roman poet Martial. I must have shown Eddie some of these, because in 1997, he wrote:

Keep the Martial torch burning. It seems to me it could make a very attractive *Morning Star* production so I hope Alec Finlay takes it up.

I can't remember if I *did* send them to Eck Finlay. In the end, however, they were taken up by Anne Thomson's admirable Galdragon Press and published as two lovely hand-printed booklets. Meanwhile, Eddie congratulated me on my 'half-century':

Have no fear of the wonders to come. Do I not see you
sipping sherry in an eventide home on the Mare Seren-
itatis in 2047, admiring the earthrise?'

I wish! In another letter that same year, re Martial, Eddie said:

Does and goat both good. In reply I enclose a recent
piece, further east than Rome.

Did I think that if he could send me poems, it was OK to send
him some of mine as well? It looks as though I became gradually less shy about sharing. We seem to have been communi-
cating as fellow poets, not just as hero and acolyte.

I had a group of love poems published by Gael Turnbull,
Sappho Said It (minimal missive, 2002). Eddie wrote:

I'm enjoying your minimal missive. Ah, those lad-
dered tights: that's the thing. But the initial Sappho
poem is too.

Finally, I showed him one particular love poem where he said
if I cut the last line I'd have 'a perfect poem'. I was very keen
on that last line. But what do you do when Edwin Morgan suggests cutting it? I cut it.

Sometimes he could be punctiliously literal. He once took
me to task for saying in a poem that an osprey was being
mobbed by a crow. 'A mob is more than one.'

I was surprised at this literalness, this querying of what I
thought was legitimate poetic licence. That time, though, I
kept the solecism.

To tell the truth, I'm not sure Eddie liked many of my 'I'
poems. He wanted me to stretch my imagination sometimes,
get away from the merely observational (*he* should talk!). He
was warmer about poems such as my slightly surreal 'Robin's
Cruise', a non-realistic poem without me in it. I have to push
myself to do these things.

012 OBG 12-4-1989

I've heard of Leda and
the swan, but Orpheus
and the pelican ———!
    My buzzer, you will
be glad to know, is
loud and clear again.
    The man said I had a
fine wire fault, which I
daresay is better than having
a coarse wire fault.
        Till Sunday.

THE NATIONAL GALLERY

HAMISH WHYTE

3 MARISCAT ROAD

GLASGOW G41 4ND

19P

9. Nothing Not Giving Messages

As well as co-editing with Robert Crawford *About Edwin Morgan*, a collection of essays on Eddie's work, to coincide with his seventieth birthday in 1990, I decided I should make use of my by now huge mass of Morgan material. I began to quarry the books, pamphlets, magazines and ephemera I had gathered, to put together a book of reprinted pieces by Eddie: interviews, talks, broadcasts, articles, statements, etc, from 1959 to 1989, covering his work as poet, translator, critic and academic.

The result was *Nothing Not Giving Messages: reflections on work and life* (Polygon, 1990). I took the title from a comment Eddie had made in an interview with Crawford: 'Nothing is not giving messages, I think.' This was, I felt, a tenet central to his work—everything has a story to tell. The cover was a collage incorporating images from Eddie's scrapbooks, held in Glasgow University Library. My editor was the brilliant Peter Kravitz.

As with the bibliography, Eddie followed this project closely, correcting many a slip of tongue and pen, without interfering with the general shape of the book. He had said he would never write an autobiography—I believe Michael Schmidt of Carcanet asked him once—his life, he said, was in the poems—so I wondered if this book might be considered as notes toward an autobiographical volume. I also had the idea it might be fun to 'interview' not the man but his Glasgow flat, and use this as the book's introduction.

So on the fourth of July 1989, I arrived at Whittinghame Court with my notebook and took a kind of inventory of the rooms, like a literary estate agent, with Eddie following me round and making comments as we went.

It was a fascinating journey about the house. What messages could Eddie's home, like all homes, be giving?

As well as an amazing collection of books and art, I saw triggers for poems, such as the trilobites—now on my mantelpiece—and the city balcony and the French windows—site of 'Strawberries'; the brass Chinese dragon—now in possession of his friend Mark (see 'Dragon on Watch' in *Love and a Life*); photographs of lovers, especially John Scott; homely articles like a blue tin of sewing stuff ('if a button comes off'), Eddie's mother's brush and mirror set, a gleaming brass four-gospels bell ('my woman's mad for brass'); the dining table by the window he preferred to work at ('I discovered I liked a view when writing'); an origami house made for him by my daughter; the little-used study with its three-legged teak desk from Lewis's department store—now in the Scottish Poetry Library; and finishing the tour in the bedroom with its medallion of the Hindu god Ganesha ('very good luck').

I didn't list anything in the bathroom, the bleakest room in the house, with no books or pictures: nothing there really but some shaving stuff, toothpaste (Euthymol) and brush—a cold room. The loo paper, as I had noticed before, was Izal Germicide, sheets in a cardboard dispenser—the stuff I remembered from my childhood and which Eddie's parents probably had as well. Very retro. And as uncomfortable as ever.

This listing (without the bathroom) was published in the book as 'About the House' (stealing Auden's title). I also included a transcription of 'Books I Have Read 1927-1940', a list Eddie meticulously kept in an old Letts's Pocket Diary for 1933 (around eight hundred volumes).

But the highlight of the volume was a previously unpublished interview (actually a conflation of two interviews) with the poet and novelist Christopher Whyte (no relation), which had been conducted in 1988. Eddie had shown me a transcript of the interview and I immediately wanted to include it in the book.

Christopher's idea, for a project of his own, was to explore Eddie's gay life and writing and their background. Using a phrase from the interview, I called the chapter 'Power from things not declared', since central to the interview was discussion about Eddie writing at a time when homosexuality was illegal and when Eddie might have lost his university post if it had been discovered he was gay—and how such tensions might contribute to the poems.

We agreed that publication of the interview was timely. Eddie was okay with this public exposure and confirmation of his sexuality. Of course, most of Eddie's friends and the poetry community (as it's called now) were aware of Eddie's sexual orientation but it was not widely known. I remember in 1983 when I was including Eddie's poems in my anthology

Noise and Smoky Breath saying to the director of the Third Eye Centre, 'Did you not know Eddie's gay?' He was flabbergasted.

Interestingly, the Iain Crichton Smith article on Eddie's love poems in *About Edwin Morgan* made no reference to the fact that they were all addressing men. Robert Crawford and I asked him to rewrite it but he refused, as if he found it difficult to acknowledge his friend's sexuality. I would like to think that he subscribed to what was Eddie's own outlook on his poems.

Asked in the interview with Christopher Whyte whether he was writing for a gay audience, Eddie replied:

> I don't take it from that angle. I'd probably just say I'm a writer, I write poetry, it's meant for anybody who takes it up to get what he or she can out of it.

Whatever—Eddie, at seventy, felt ready to come out publicly.

We didn't, however, realise the fuss that this would cause. I was phoned by John Linklater of *The Glasgow Herald* and was taken aback to be asked if I thought Eddie's coming out as gay would harm his reputation. I wasn't sure what to say and blurted out, 'Well, it didn't do Auden any harm, did it?'

The Christopher Whyte interview was also moving because Eddie talked for the first time in detail about John Scott and their relationship, a relationship that lasted sixteen years. It ended in a trivial quarrel that was never resolved before John died—which Eddie bitterly regretted for the rest of his life (it's a recurring motif in his poems from the late 1970s on). They had met in Green's Playhouse cinema in Glasgow where, incidentally, I had my first date with Winifred. It was a great place for assignations, gay and straight.

Throughout the years I knew Eddie, John was mentioned occasionally but never at length. Eddie sometimes talked about the holidays they spent together. The photograph of him smoking—he was a heavy smoker (see 'One Cigarette')—was prominent in Eddie's sitting room. He was a presence.

10. Editing Eddie (The Mariscat Years)

1982–2002

As already mentioned, Eddie played a seminal role in the setting up of the Mariscat Press: 'Mariscat would be a fine name.'

The proto-publication of his nine one-word poems wasn't really a serious proposition. But it was a germ. Later that year (1982), my friend Kevin McCarra suggested it might be a good idea to publish David Neilson's Glaswegian translations of Catullus, which we both admired.

And so, as described earlier, the pamphlet *XII from Catullus* became the first public production of the press—and received an endorsement from Eddie, no less, who commented on these 'rude and reductive versions' in his essay 'Glasgow Speech in Recent Scottish Literature' the following year.

And, as I have recounted in *Cat's Whiskers: 30 Years of Mariscat Press* (2012), the publishing bug bit and Mariscat has now published over a hundred items: books, pamphlets, cards, by writers such as Gael Turnbull, Douglas Dunn, Janice Galloway, Michael Longley, A.L. Kennedy, Jackie Kay, Brian McCabe, Fiona Pitt-Kethley, Anna Crowe, Jane McKie, Diana Hendry, Tom Pow, Stewart Conn, Michèle Roberts, Lesley Glaister, Alyson Hallett, Alison Prince, Christine De Luca and Richie McCaffery, among others, including twelve by Eddie—maybe not much in general publishing history terms, but both Kevin and I were working full-time for most of the period.

By the end of 1982 I was well into compiling the bibliography and getting to know Eddie better. What more natural extension to recording his work than to publish it as well? Kevin particularly admired Eddie's poem 'Grendel', about the monster from Beowulf (Eddie loved these literary creatures— see his poems on Caliban, Ariel and Puck, for example). We thought 'Grendel' would make a good poem-card to distribute at Christmas and help publicise the press. Eddie was happy to go along with this.

With a nod to private press ethos, we decided to have the poem hand-printed. I enlisted Stephen Gill of Arran Gallery Press, and asked an artist friend, Peter Harrison, to provide an illustration. The result was a handsome card, printed in red and black on Heritage Book White in an edition of three hundred. To our (and Eddie's) annoyance, Stephen was so excited by the project that he printed all three hundred copies before Eddie's final proof corrections had been made—he had to run it through the press again with a *corrigendum*. Nonetheless, we were all happy with the result.

I got a phone call from Tom Fenton (brother of James) of the prestigious Salamander Press who had come across the card, admired it and wanted to order ten copies. This was endorsement indeed and we felt the press could be a going concern. We also had praise from Alan Tarling of the Poet & Printer press, a favourite of mine.

Eddie obviously considered we were now a *bona fide* outfit and was very pleased to have a local publisher, particularly for more experimental or small-scale works that his main publisher Carcanet might not consider separately. So he was keen for us to do something more and began to offer us ideas. The first we took up was a new batch of *Instamatic Poems*, his snapshot poems based on press reports, written after the first had been published ten years earlier.

Then in June 1982, Eddie sent me a copy of his sonnet 'The Solway Canal', picturing a future Scotland separated from England (I still have it, a carbon copy on thin quarto-sized paper, signed with Eddie's monogram). I was immediately excited by this—what a fascinating idea!—and suggested he write more sonnets, in the form of a sequence of postcards sent from an imagined future Scotland. Eddie wrote back:

> When I wrote 'The Solway Canal' I had the vague idea of making it the first of a series, and when you made the same suggestion ... this must have given the necessary jog.

Needless to say, the result wildly exceeded my modest proposal. Six more 'Sonnets from Scotland' appeared and we printed them in the first issue of *The Glasgow Magazine*, which Kevin and I had started in 1982 with some friends (Tom Berry, David Neilson and Alasdair Robertson). I should here confess, to my shame, that one of the sonnets was printed with a misspelled title. We issued an erratum slip—which also got it wrong—and had to issue an erratum to the erratum! My cheeks still burn.

Strangely, just as Eddie had been in at the beginning of the Mariscat Press, he had been unwittingly present at the conception of *The Glasgow Magazine.* I was having lunch in the Horseshoe pub in Glasgow with my architect friend Tom Berry. We were at the bar with our Guinness and macaroni cheese and Tom was saying we needed a new magazine, how about starting one up of our own. I agreed, then turned to go off to the loo, when I spotted Eddie sitting at a side table with a chap. I was careful not to acknowledge his presence; I thought he would prefer that. I'm sure he saw me as well, but it was never mentioned by either of us. I suppose it was a kind of unspoken secret. So, he was again in the background to another literary project.

Anyway, Kevin and I wondered about publishing the sonnets along with the Instamatics. We thought it would be a good gimmick to print the book with the two collections back to back. Eddie was tickled with this idea and wrote to me on 27 August 1982:

> Your idea of a back-to-back book quite appeals. I have one such on my shelves, a paperback with JUNKIE by 'William Lee' (i.e. William Burroughs—his first book, I believe?) at one end and Maurice Helbrant's NARCOTIC AGENT at the other, in a series of such 'Double Books' published by Ace in New York in the 1950s. When you've read the first half you turn the book upside-down and start again, reading from left to right in the usual way. The covers are designed so that there are really two fronts, not a front and a back. (Equally lurid too, I may add?) As for the contents, the Instamatics would be fine for one half, but I would prefer something other than SONNETS FROM SCOTLAND for the other half: these are still going forward (fifteen at the moment) and I would rather wait till the sequence is finished and publish it by itself if possible. I wondered if it might be a good idea to combine the Instamatics with the so-far-untitled poems (also 20 in number) grown from fragments supplied by Michael

Schmidt. Both groups start from defined external données (newspaper item; a line or two of abandoned poetry) and they could be linked perhaps by a title for the book like GRAFTS AND TAKES, 'takes' still including the Instamatic idea but also suggesting the taking of grafts. I know MS is quite happy for me to publish the 'grafts' under my own name, since they are virtually my poems (there was no collaboration), so long as we have a brief explanatory note. See what you and Kevin think—I am enclosing the 29 poems so that you can see them as a group ... Alasdair Gray sounds an excellent idea for a cover/covers.

Not all authors take such care and have such an eye for detail.

We published 300 copies of *Grafts/Takes*, 26 of them cloth-bound, lettered and signed, and 274 in paperback. It was printed by Eddie Peterson of South Shields, an excellent printer recommended by Chris Carrell, Director of the Third Eye Centre. Alasdair Gray's cover design was a double line-portrait of the author, each slightly different—his face stares fiercely out at the reader twice. Eddie didn't like it, although he recognised its striking quality.

Jim McGonigal in his biography of Edwin Morgan, *Beyond the Last Dragon*, analyses the proportion of contributions to the *Grafts* by each author, and concludes there was more Schmidt than Eddie admitted. He suggests Eddie 'had a problem with the give and take of poetic partnerships'—a problem I have to say I never encountered when we were to-ing and fro-ing with our sequence *Wild Cuts* many years later; and Eddie did *say* there was no collaboration between him and Michael. However, I would agree that, as Jim writes, 'A certain self-centredness is often a useful quality in a major artistic talent.'

One of the stories I often tell when talking about Mariscat (and publishing in general) concerns the spine of *Grafts/Takes*. Looking at the spine one way, it reads: EDWIN MORGAN GRAFTS. When you turn it round, it reads: MARISCAT PRESS TAKES. And that sums up the relationship between authors and the publishing industry! The nineteenth century poet Thomas Campbell allegedly wrote: 'Now Barabbas was a publisher.'

In those early days of the press, Kevin and I got a definite thrill from bagging a major poet for Mariscat. I suppose it's the ultimate fandom—not only meeting your favourite writer but publishing them as well. We had also attracted another favourite major (to us, anyway) poet to our list—Gael Turnbull. Again, this was someone pleased to have a Scottish publisher. Kevin and I arranged a meeting with both Gael and Eddie (who knew each other slightly) in the coffee shop of the Burrell Collection in Pollok Park on Glasgow's south side. We could hardly believe our luck, innocent publishing newbies that we were. There we were, sitting at the same table as two of our favourite poets. How smug we felt. Gael also became a good friend.

The book of which we were to become the proudest came out the following year. Eddie finally let us get our hands on *Sonnets from Scotland*. This was a more serious publication and we all gave it much careful thought. As supporters of Scottish independence, and in the wake of the failed devolution referendum of 1979, we wanted it to be defiantly Scottish. I chose Scotch Roman as the typeface and Alasdair Gray's blue and white cover design featured vignettes of some of the subjects of the poems (as well as a new version of our cat device) interspersed with saltires. And we launched it on St Andrew's Night, 30 November 1984, in the Mitchell Library.

The following Saturday afternoon Eddie gave a reading of the complete sequence of fifty sonnets to a packed audience at the Third Eye Centre in Sauchiehall Street. Kevin and I asked the Centre staff if we could record the reading and they agreed. I'm not sure what we intended to do with the recording, but we did feel that it was an important occasion—historic, even.

In the event the Third Eye's tape machine failed to record (a dud tape I think) and a great (marathon) reading was lost to posterity. Kevin has always had the motto, 'let it go', so we weren't too bothered. The book sold well and we reprinted, with some of the rave press reviews on the back cover replacing the *hors serie* sonnet Eddie had written for me about Mariscat, and it won a Scottish Arts Council Award.

We were so proprietorial over the sonnets that when Carcanet wanted to include the sequence in Eddie's *Themes on a Variation* in 1988, we asked for—and got—a reprint fee. This was the only time we did so, the unwritten agreement being that we would publish smaller collections, mainly sequences, which would later be subsumed into larger Carcanet collections. We still have the satisfaction of having published *Sonnets from Scotland* first.

Our concentration on poetic sequences or series by Eddie continued with his reflections on developing visual technology—*From the Video Box*, 1986. Based on Channel 4's *Right to Reply*, in which viewers could record themselves and their opinions, it was a series of monologues commenting on imagined television programmes—a wide range: from a woman looking for her cat to the final of the world jigsaw competition—the latter becoming a favourite of poets in particular.

In 1988 we brought out another sequence, limericks this time, about animals, from the amoeba to the zebu: *Tales from Limerick Zoo*. These pieces of light verse have never been included in any other collection and I suppose they could now be a collector's item. They may be light verse, but the circumstances of their composition were anything but light.

Eddie had been keeping an eye on his aunt, Myra Parrot, his mother's sister, who lived in the same block of flats. She was becoming confused and had actually begun to accuse him of stealing things from her flat (a common feature of dementia). This was a worrying period, and unable to write anything else and to keep himself calm and his mind occupied, Eddie started jotting down these verses at different times and places: waiting for a bus, at the airport, anywhere—a kind of therapy.

We published the limericks as a pamphlet with witty black and white illustrations by David Neilson. This was against our usual dislike of illustrated poems, but it seemed a reasonable exception and broke up the regiment of verse.

Tales from Limerick Zoo was launched at one of the strangest readings I have ever attended. It was at the Third Eye Centre, on a rainy night in November. It was ostensibly a Polish Night, with readings by visiting poets from Poland and from Tom Leonard and Eddie.

Tom read, very badly, a long, terrible poem by Thomas Campbell, 'Lines on Poland', and Eddie read his limericks—totally out of place—and one of the Polish poets had a heated public spat with his translator in the middle of his reading.

A memorable evening. Eddie's post-event postcard two days later asked, 'How did you enjoy the Polish shambles?' Also, his eagle eye had 'Just noticed a mistake in the limericks:

> [...] second line of 'Ibis' should have 'the book', not 'a book'. (Dittography again presumably, from the first line?) Perfection, elusive nymph, keeps slipping away—.

He kept us on our typo toes.

And so the cycle of sequences went on: *Hold Hands Among the Atoms* (1991)—the set of 'social' poems he wrote for his seventieth birthday in 1990; *The Maker on High* (1997), a translation of a poem by St Columba, which we had hand-printed in a limited edition by David Hamilton at his Partick Press. By this time Kevin had left for London to work for *The Guardian* and I continued on my own, publishing mainly pamphlets by a variety of poets.

Eddie continued to delight and challenge. *Demon*, written between January 1998 and January 1999, was an astonishing series of twenty poems featuring another alter ego, the restless, driven demon, always on the move ('go / is all I know'), who weaves in and out of time and space, interrogating, antagonising and trying to kill death—utterly fascinating, not least in the light of Eddie's cancer diagnosis in the summer of 1999. Some regard these poems as among his best.

Demon was a striking-looking pamphlet. The jacket design featured a strange medieval figure (I had found it somewhere in the library) combined with the title in Eddie's own distinctive handwriting. He showed his usual interest in the production. He wrote on 25 June:

> *Demon* proofs returned with quite a few corrections. Will you have a good look at the corrections yourself, in case they aren't always clear. On the Auschwitz problem: perhaps it would be best to keep Oswiecim accentless rather than risk some desperate approximation? Perpetua looks good.

Ever since our first publication, translation has been an interest and an irregular feature for Mariscat. In 2001, we published translations by Eddie of one of his favourite poets, the

Hungarian Attila Jozsef. It was launched at the Kibble Palace, the great glasshouse in Glasgow's Botanic Gardens, on a sea of Bull's Blood wine, with music by my White Street Band (mazurkas and polkas were the closest we managed to appropriate tunes).

In 2002, Mariscat was pleased to have a joint publication with Carcanet. This was *Cathures,* a Glasgow-centred collection, including the poems written by Eddie as Glasgow's first Poet Laureate. The cover illustration was a moody photograph of the city by my son Kenny, who was very happy to have this first professional use of his hobby—and to be paid for it!

Between September and November 2002, despite cancer and the ongoing treatment beginning to take their toll, Eddie kept up a busy schedule: regular lunches with me; the visit to David Daiches for his ninetieth birthday; reading at Glasgow Gallery of Modern Art (again supported by my band) for National Poetry Day; the Goethe Institut for a special showing of the German silent film *Der Golem,* with myself and fellow film buff Stuart Airlie (husband of Robyn Marsack of the Scottish Poetry Library) followed by dinner at the *Rogano*; lengthy recorded interviews with myself and Alan Riach, of the Department of Scottish Literature at Glasgow University (notionally for a biography); attending a Mariscat twentieth birthday bash at the Mitchell Library; and launching *Cathures* at Borders bookshop.

And, despite all this, or maybe because (he worked best in busyness), he also completed the fifty-poem sequence, *Love and a Life* (this time, variations on a theme). He found himself working on this amazingly frank and revelatory series of poems nearly every day and, as he said, 'with considerable excitement.' In an interview with Phil Miller of *The Herald* he commented:

> I honestly don't know how I started writing this, but
> I got very excited about the ideas. There's something
> about autumn that made me think back and take stock
> of my life.

An unaccustomed direction for Eddie to look.

After the frenzy of writing *Love and a Life* had died down and he realised what he had actually written, Eddie began to have doubts. He initially felt that the poems shouldn't be published until after his death—he worried they were too personal, too raw; and they named names. He asked me what to do. I was his friend as well as his publisher. So of course I said they should be published. I thought he had nothing to fear.

The launch of *Love and a Life* at Borders bookshop in Glasgow on 27 May 2003 was Eddie's last major public appearance before entering a care home. He was eighty-three. It was a memorable event.

The printer had been somewhat dilatory (printers' disease) but we had managed to secure enough advance copies for the launch (hastily bound, many of them fell apart later). Eddie held the large audience—mainly young people, all clutching their copies snapped up before the reading—absolutely entranced with this honest autobiographical journey through his life and loves.

Beforehand, I had dared Eddie to read the most sexually explicit poems—and he did. He was a brave man—and mischievous (he knew about shock value). There was a smaller gathering at the Scottish Poetry Library on 5 July to celebrate the book. And that was his last reading in public.

Mariscat published two more of his books: *Tales from Baron Munchausen* in 2005 and the last book before he died, the only Mariscat 'miscellaneous' collection (rather than a series or sequence), a retrospective: *Dreams and Other Nightmares: New and Uncollected Poems* 1954–2009. The latter was launched on 27 April 2010 at a reception in the Mitchell Library to celebrate his ninetieth birthday—a warm gathering. He managed to cut his cake (which had a spaceship on it) and friends read some of his poems. He was also able to sign a few copies. At the end, as I was helping him into the taxi taking him back to Clarence Court care home, he said, with satisfaction, 'A good turnout!' Numbers always mattered.

◆

EM, HW, Kevin McCarra (holding a Wild Thing), Susan Stewart, Mariscat Road, 1993
(Winifred Whyte)

Winifred, Whittinghame Court, 8 January 1995 (HW)

EM pouring absinthe, Whittinghame Court, 26 November 2001 (HW)

HW and EM, Kibble Palace, 27 April 2000: 80th birthday bash (Kenny Whyte)

Kevin McCarra and EM, Mitchell Library, 28 October 2002: Mariscat Press 20th birthday celebration (HW)

EM and HW, Kibble Palace, 27 April 2000: 80th birthday bash (Kenny Whyte)

HW, Robyn Marsack and EM, Kibble Palace, 27 April 2000: launch of *Unknown is Best* at 80th birthday bash (Kenny Whyte)

Marshall Walker and EM, Glasgow City Halls, 7 September 1997 (HW)

HW and EM, Bath Street, 23 March 2001 (Hartmut Salmen)

HW, Claudia Kraszkiewicz, EM and Steven Campbell, Edinburgh, 25 October 2001: after press launch of 'A Tribute to Edwin Morgan' at the National Portrait Gallery (Hartmut Salmen)

HW and EM, *Yes* restaurant, 12 October 2002 (Hartmut Salmen)

HW and EM, Lynedoch House, Bearsden, 16 February 2004: installation of EM as Scots Makar

EM, HW and Jim McGonigal, Clarence Court

EM and HW, Clarence Court, April 2005: birthday visit—present of a beaded curtain
(Valerie Thornton)

Diana and Hamish (Muna Whyte)

EM, Renfrew Ferry, 5 May 1990: 70th birthday bash (HW)

Through his writing life, Eddie's writing methods were consistent. He was generally a pencil and paper man (often with a clipboard) and then he transferred the work to his Blue Bird typewriter (which he'd had adapted to include accents). He would let things simmer in his head for a while, then he would get them down, writing fast, with few changes. You just need to look at almost any manuscript by him to see the truth of this. There would inevitably be some changes to be made when typing from manuscript—it seems impossible to avoid. Editing is endemic to writers.

In many ways, editing Eddie—through all the publications we did together—was easy. When he presented his text to you, it was pretty well set. You could try arguing with him if there was something you thought not quite right, but he was usually determined on the text as was. Occasionally you could persuade him of the odd point—more often something minor, punctuation or the like. Never on vocabulary, as I found out the hard way early on. He meant what he wrote. He expected you to accept the text as delivered.

What he *was* interested in, and was willing to discuss, was the matter of presentation—that always seemed to be at the forefront. Witness the interest he showed, as described earlier, in the format of *Grafts/Takes*. He always wanted to know how the poems would be shown off: format, typography, cover illustration, etc. And when it came to proof-reading, I don't think I've ever come across an author with a sharper eye—as Robyn Marsack, his sometime editor at Carcanet and no mean proof reader herself—can also testify.

I had often made suggestions about what poems might be included in a book, but after Eddie moved into a care home (and as his cancer progressed), I played a bigger part in putting together his two final collections, one from Carcanet and the other from Mariscat. If physically he wasn't able to gather and arrange poems, his mental interest and care—and delight— were undiminished. I had thought of including the whole of the sequence 'Planet Wave' in what was to become *A Book of Lives*. This was Eddie's 'short history of the world' (after H. G. Wells), which had never been published in its complete form.

In *Beyond the Last Dragon*, Jim McGonigal reports that I asked Eddie in a letter, 'Are we including Planet Wave I (as well as II)? The full boorach?' and goes into an explanation and derivation of the word 'boorach' from the Gaelic for 'heap' or 'crowd'. I'm flattered, but I think Jim has misread my terrible handwriting. In fact, I wrote 'The full boonah', using the Glaswegian expression for the whole lot—though Jim's interpretation is possibly more interesting.

Eddie never liked explanatory notes in his books of poems. He always said that his strong inclination was 'to non-pamper the reader'. He wore his learning fairly lightly but it was a wide learning. 'Readers can look things up if they want to know,' he said. I did, nonetheless, manage to persuade him of the usefulness of biographical notes at the back of *A Book of Lives* and an index to *Sonnets from Scotland*, both of which I compiled.

We first discussed the *Book of Lives* collection in October 2005 and worked on it over the following year. We got proofs from Carcanet in December 2006 and the book was published in February 2007. The cover design is a clever configuration of Morganesque. I had suggested an illustration of portraits (a book of lives) from the *Liber Chronicarum*, the first illustrated history of the world, published in Nuremberg in 1493. Eddie wasn't keen—'too medieval' he said.)

But what the Carcanet designer Stephen Raw did was to replace the portraits of the medieval people with words—phrases, names, nouns—taken from Eddie's poems themselves and arrange them in a kind of structure of related cells, on a background of what looked suspiciously like dried blood, or clusters of constellations—Rimbaud, Babel, Twin Towers, flame, music, hydrogen, Gorbals, Sputnik, etc—all genes, as it were, of human history, given a home and a voice by Eddie. The book was a Poetry Book Society Choice and the selectors commented that it was 'muscular to an extent that feels almost medieval in his use of form'.

The final book from Mariscat, *Dreams and Other Nightmares*, wasn't so straightforward. Its main purpose was to publish the poems based on a series of nightmares experienced by Eddie towards the end of 2007 and which Jim McGonigal helped put into shape, as he describes in fascinating detail in his biography. There were seven of them—hardly enough for a pamphlet, never mind a book—but Eddie and I were both keen to see them in print, although only four of them made the final cut.

I wondered about adding a gathering of uncollected (and even some unpublished) poems from across his whole writing life, to provide a retrospective, a kind of summing up. Unspoken was the understanding that this would be his last book.

So Jim worked with Eddie on the dream poems, and supplied me with poems he'd come across in Eddie's papers in the Special Collections Department of Glasgow University Library. Meanwhile, I began digging into my own papers, and elsewhere, for other poems, including uncollected work from earlier Mariscat publications, notably *Hold Hands Among the Atoms*. For me, this was a pleasurable bibliographical excursion: I was still collecting Morganiana with a view to updating my 1990 checklist. I had plenty of material to sift through.

I photocopied a large pile of poems and gave them to Eddie to have a look at. Then I spent a happy afternoon with him going through them. Looking back, I think it was one of our closest moments, that quiet thumbing-through of poems, the rustle of paper, his quiet comments. I would hand each poem to him and he would read it while I waited for his verdict.

His remarks went like this: 'Yes.' 'No.' 'That's a good one' (in surprised tone). 'I don't remember this!' (again surprised).

What he *really* thought, seeing poems brought back to the light after fifty years of writing, I don't know. But this is the kind of experience that makes editing and publishing so worthwhile and, in this instance, curiously moving.

We weren't sure what would be a suitable cover design. My son Kenny had supplied the cover photograph for *Cathures*, so I asked him for more pictures to consider. The image Eddie finally chose was a black and white photograph (interesting for a man who preferred colour). It showed a detail of a wrought iron gate at Castle Howard in Yorkshire (a favourite haunt of Kenny and his wife Muna—and I seem to remember it appearing in one of Eddie's poems), with a spider's web white with frost. Kenny had mirror-imaged the photograph, giving it a symmetrical look. This worked well for a cover and its overprinting of text. Eddie wondered if the viewer was entering by this gate or leaving—nicely ambiguous. To me the design echoed the emotive (and, as it happened, apposite) poem in the collection, 'Heaven' (originally in *Grafts/Takes*):

[...] And keys at the gate! Incredible! Rings of them,
ancient, made of metal, for each arriver—
and no instructions to find your own place.
We have had too many nightmares
not to know that winding drive
that grows darker and darker
overhung with rhododendrons.
Shaking, we follow it
to the black, mossed porch.
The house is derelict.
We tiptoe up the stair
to the last room
with the last key
and get it to growl
round in its hole
and let us push into
paradise, paradise
please, if we may.

11. Safaris

I Memories

On Sunday 7 September 1997, I found myself in the back seat of a white VW Golf, a kind of piggy in the middle, with Eddie as the front passenger and his old friend Marshall Walker as driver, racketing about Glasgow, following our own Edwin Morgan Heritage Trail.

This was the first of two Morgan safaris to places in Glasgow and environs associated with Eddie's early life and poems: a trip down memory lane for Eddie and, for Marshall and myself, a biographical mapping session. Marshall, a former colleague of Eddie's at Glasgow University, was on sabbatical from Waikato University in New Zealand, where he'd been appointed Professor of English in 1981. He had borrowed his son's car for the day.

I first met Marshall when I was putting together the exhibition at the Mitchell Library for Eddie's sixtieth birthday in April 1980. Eddie must have told him about the exhibition. Into the Glasgow Room marched this ebullient character who asked the instantly alienating question, 'Do you know who I am?' I remember bridling.

He told me he was Eddie's executor and he wanted to have a look at what was going into the display. I suppose he was checking it out in his role as guardian of the flame. So I showed him the display cases. He then said—presumably realising this was a serious project—that he would like to donate to the library the typescript of an interview he'd conducted with Eddie five years earlier.

I softened at this point, and it was the beginning of an amicable relationship. I didn't see much of him over the following years as he was teaching in New Zealand, but we did meet now and then, especially after Kevin McCarra and I had agreed to join him as more local co-executors.

As the 1990s wore on and Eddie approached the age of eighty, Marshall became a little anxious about what might happen after Eddie's death and the three of us discussed this at length—reluctantly, of course. We even looked at venues for a memorial event: the Mitchell Theatre seemed the most suitable. And what about a biography? Kevin and I thought Marshall was the obvious biographer, but he wasn't keen. He particularly seemed to shy away from the gay side of Eddie's life, which Kevin and I thought a bit surprising, but maybe not—Marshall was such a heterosexually macho man.

Whatever his reasons, he was a good and loyal friend. Despite saying he wouldn't write a biography, he did suggest he become a kind of biographical timekeeper for Eddie, keeping a record of Eddie's doings as a useful function of being an executor. They met several times to set down background. In a letter (18 June 1998) Marshall told me

> [...] after I came to NZ, he would send me, at my prompting, a sort of annual digest of his diary.

From this, Marshall compiled a timeline of Eddie's life, which proved very useful to James McGonigal when he came to write the biography. Up to the early 1980s, Marshall's record contains much biographical information (some of it based on our 1997 safari), but the mode then changes to more of a listing of activities and publications. It runs to 1997. It does make one wonder at Eddie's motives in encouraging all this record-keeping—was a bibliography not enough? Was there a passion to be remembered? A neurosis, even? In any event, it was Marshall who suggested we go exploring the places of Eddie's past.

And so, fairly early that September morning we rendez-voused at my flat in Mariscat Road, Pollokshields. Winifred gave us all coffee and home-made scones, we sketched out a very rough route, and set off.

Our first stop was 245 Nithsdale Road, Pollokshields, opposite Sherbrooke St Gilbert's church, where the Morgan family moved from Hyndland in 1922—from a tenement flat to a substantial, red sandstone, semi-detached villa. This was the district where Eddie's parents had lived before they were married. Eddie himself lived here until he was eight years old.

We all got out of the car and Eddie allowed himself, after a slight reluctance, to be photographed standing at the gate of 245. He said this was the place of his earliest memories. He recalled his delight in the trees above his pram. He remembered the neighbours' dog and how he was afraid of it—'it flew at me once'—but this didn't put him off dogs. He talked about his father who had been deaf from youth and who would get upset because he thought people were laughing at him.

We then drove a short distance to Larch Road, Dumbreck, where Eddie attended a private primary school in the 1920s. He couldn't remember what it looked like, so Marshall marched up and down the paths of the more imposing buildings, ringing the bells and asking residents if they knew anything about the school. Nobody did. I later looked it up in the library and discovered it was at 'Roskene', 21 Larch Road, a modest terraced house, and run by a Miss Mary L. Ross. (When I told Eddie about this he said the name was faintly familiar, but he didn't have a mental picture of her.)

As we were casting about for the right place, Eddie told us that when he was about six, he and a girl called Violet were first equal in a test. 'Violet got the prize as well: she must have been very clever!' He also remembered making things with plasticine and the taste of glitter wax. Sensory memories do seem to last the longest.

Giving up on finding the school, we drove on and passed 11 Maxwell Drive, Pollokshields, where Eddie's mother's parents had lived. Their house was long gone and new houses put up. Mr and Mrs Arnott were keen gardeners and Eddie remembered their 'scented garden'. Sweet peas were his favourite flowers—he loved their scent ('Sweet pea mignonette wallflower phlox', in 'An Early Garden'). In his last years it was a delight to see the pleasure he took in a posy I brought to him in his care home room. 'Ah! Sweet peas!'

And so to Burnside, where Eddie lived with his parents from about 1928 until 1962 when he moved to his flat on Great Western Road at Anniesland. First, there was 10 Albert Drive (where memories came back to him of parental mealtime bickering about money); then a red sandstone bungalow at 30 Broomieknowe Road (downsizing when money was tight); and finally back to Albert Drive, this time number 12, a solid grey sandstone semi-detached Victorian villa (now a Church of Scotland manse).

Marshall and I took photographs of the houses. All Eddie said, looking round, was 'Happy days.' I'm sure we were hoping for more than minimal responses, but he wasn't to be drawn. We kept bombarding him with questions—where? why? how?—all Kipling's six servants. I found out later that Eddie, aged about eight or nine had played in goal for the Albertonians in the local street league. He wasn't a sporty type.

The next stop was Stonelaw School in Rutherglen, formerly Rutherglen Academy, as it was when Eddie attended in the 1930s. Perhaps Eddie was growing ever more uneasy about the enterprise: at this point he absolutely refused to get out of the car. So I stayed with him while Marshall scampered about and climbed railings to photograph the rather ugly building.

'I hated it', said Eddie, and added that he thought the standard of teaching there was 'pretty awful'. He was mocked on his first day for wearing shoes with buckles (everyone else had lace-ups)—he got 'normal' footwear after that.

But it wasn't all bad. He was encouraged in his writing by his English teacher, Mr Hutcheon, a 'small peppery man' who embarrassed young Eddie by insisting on walking home from school with him, talking about literature. As we drove through Rutherglen on the way back to Glasgow Eddie suddenly remembered the Cross Café, a local haunt.

We diverted to Candleriggs in town to see the poems by Eddie that had been cut into the pavement outside the City Halls. They didn't look too well cared for and proved difficult to photograph. Marshall, in his usual insouciant way, scaled the wrought iron gates for an aerial view. Two people stopped to read the poems. There was a feather lying on one of them, but we didn't remove it.

GHOSTLY WORKERS SLEEP BELOW
THEY HEAR NO RAIN OR HEEL AND TOE
THINK OF THEM WHERE THE FORGES GLOW
IN THE GLASGOW OF LONG AGO

PRAISE FOR THE TREE THAT GROWLED BUT GREW
PRAISE FOR THE BIRD THAT FAINTED BUT FLEW
PRAISE FOR THE BELL THAT RUSTED BUT RANG
PRAISE FOR THE FISH THAT SIGHED BUT SWAM

They were signed with Eddie's monogram: three horizontal and three vertical lines cut into the stone.

We had a pleasant lunch break at the Babbity Bowster restaurant, where I was sure I saw the President of the Burns Federation slurping (favourite word of Eddie's) a bowl of cullen skink.

The end of our day's safari was Eddie's beginning. This was 60 Novar Drive, Hyndland, in the west of the city, where he was born in 1920, though it was called York Drive then. It's a street of red sandstone tenements, with green and pink art nouveau tiles and dark wooden bannisters in the closes. There were no memories here, but Eddie did recall his mother telling him how giving birth to him 'went on for ever', and so 'never again'. What a thing to tell a young child!

Marshall and I left Eddie sitting in the car reading the Sunday papers (this was the day after Princess Diana's funeral) and wandered about taking photographs and savouring the atmosphere. When we got back to the car Eddie had vanished. Absolutely no sign of him up or down the street. When Marshall tried to open the car door, we realised it was the wrong vehicle—Eddie was still sitting patiently in the right one a few yards further on.

We drove back the short distance to Eddie's flat for Glenmorangie and chat and a review of the daft day—which we had all enjoyed, perhaps Marshall and I rather more than Eddie. It *was* pleasurable, the in-car banter over my bad navigating, and Marshall's constant leaping out for snaps and checking of addresses as we followed the upwardly mobilising Morgans. I received a postcard from Eddie a few days later:

> Good teamwork yesterday, and for me a curious range
> from strong to faint recollections to the blank of Novar.

Looking back on the trip now, it's clear to me that Eddie submitted to it reluctantly, although he did enjoy certain aspects—and his curiosity, as ever, was piqued. His temperamental preference was always to concentrate on the here-and-now; the future, not the past. He may have worried about possible painful memories. He seemed uneasy being photographed beside former homes and, as I said, stubbornly refused to leave the car at his old school and in the street where he was born. So we learned more facts about him, but did we get to know him any better? We were certainly made aware of the stubbornness in his nature, that the man famous for saying 'yes' could be equally adamant about saying 'no'.

II Poems

He was definitely happier a few years later, when Claudia Kraszkiewicz (a young German student whose doctoral thesis was on Eddie's poetry, and who had set up the Edwin Morgan website along with her photographer husband Hartmut Salmen) suggested a trip round places in Glasgow associated with his poems (rather than with his life). Hartmut would take photographs for the website. This was undertaken over two days, 23 and 26 March 2001. Eddie, Claudia, Hartmut and myself were chauffeured round the sites by Jane Forrest, a writer and art facilitator I'd met through Survivors Poetry Scotland.

The five of us crammed into a small blue Ford Fiesta and, starting from Eddie's flat, we crossed Great Western Road to view Bingham's Pond ('Winter', 'The Second Life', and so on) for our first stop. We hung about in the cold while Eddie explained to Claudia the significance of the pond (swans, skaters, etc). We then headed into town, parked in Bath Street, and trooped round the corner to the Kings Café in Elmbank Street.

This café is reputedly the scene of 'In the Snack-bar', Eddie's most famous Glasgow poem—still taught in Scottish schools — a poem about his encounter with a blind hunchback. It has the formica-topped tables for cups to capsize on and two flights of stairs down to the toilets. Eddie had consistently and resolutely refused to identify the location of the poem. 'I'm not telling you,' he would say, as if determined to take at least one secret to his grave. Ultimately it doesn't matter, of course. But, going in, we asked him again. He just smiled enigmatically.

Another (possibly better) candidate for the original snack-bar was the Equi Café on Sauchiehall Street at Charing Cross: formica tables, fixed stools, stairs down. It was a favourite howf of staff at the Mitchell Library when I started work there in 1969—they did a good bacon roll.

Anyway, we needed some refreshment. Seated under the notice SPECIAL OF THE DAY HOME MADE LASAGNE we

had coffee, with scones for Eddie and me. The puzzled staff were happy to pose for Hartmut's photographs. After all, they claimed to make 'the best pizza in Town'. Just around the corner, Hartmut photographed Eddie and me in Bath Street, both of us with hats on—a photograph I treasure.

The next stop was Henderson The Jeweller in Sauchiehall Street, allegedly the scene of Eddie's instamatic poem 'Glasgow 5 March 1971' ('With a ragged diamond'). We looked at the window through which the young man and woman might have fallen backwards (or not).

Then we were off to Central Station where Eddie had seen a woman urinating on the pavement in the middle of the day ('At Central Station'). Eddie, photographer, walker-about in cities, wrote:

> the poet looks, not bold as brass
> but hard, swift, slowing his walk
> a little, accursed recorder, his feelings
> as confused as the November leaves.

It's interesting that he's not just a recorder but an 'accursed' witness—he is compelled to record, it's his job. In an interview with Alan Riach on 3 July 2000, he said:

> I feel myself to be part of it (the city). I don't feel that
> I'm just an observer, I'm actually part of this.

He always had a concern for Glasgow's vulnerable folk, as so many of his poems surely convey, and his favourite charity was Shelter. We ended the first day on Glasgow Green, the eponymous location of what Eddie came to call his early gay liberation poem. There were no sheets blowing and whipping in the sunlight, but the clothes poles were still there. The finale was a pleasant late lunch at the Inn on the Green.

We began the second day at the Gorbals Mosque ('The Gorbals Mosque'), although in the overcast morning its dome was definitely not glowing like an amulet. This was followed by a brief visit to Duke Street ('Death in Duke Street') with Hartmut snapping away, and to Rottenrow where De Quincey had once lived ('De Quincey in Glasgow') and where in the Royal Maternity Hospital—now demolished—my children, Kenny and Christina, were born).

Then we moved out of Glasgow and swung by Eddie's old family house in Burnside for just a glimpse and a photograph, before heading for Cathkin Braes. This is a parkland above Rutherglen and Burnside, where the young Eddie would go for walks when he wanted to be alone and think (as I myself did round the streets of Clarkston as a teenager) and where, later on at university, he walked, accompanied by his friend and fellow student, George Hunter. Its importance in Eddie's mythology is signalled in the title of his first collection of poems, *The Vision of Cathkin Braes*, published in 1952 when he was thirty-two.

We strolled about the place, and admired the panoramic view of Glasgow. One photograph, taken by Hartmut from above, shows Eddie alone on a grassy plain and makes one think of those lonely teenage years. But Eddie seemed happy enough to be here, where he hadn't been for many decades.

Our next stop was Riddrie Cemetery. While the grey clouds piled up, we searched and searched for the grave of William Fullarton, the violent leader of the Protestant gang of the 1930s, the Billy Boys, and the subject of Eddie's poem, 'King Billy'. We didn't find it. What we did come across was the grave of a Rangers fan, the headstone draped with a scarf in the red, white and blue team colours—this was duly photographed, for its Protestant associations. The last location was the Red Road multi-storey flats ('Glasgow Sonnet X'), to see the monoliths still standing patient, sonnets stretched to odes.

The final photograph of the journey shows Eddie in the front passenger seat of the car, his forefingers making a T— time for a break.

12. Mark

Eddie's relationship with Mark S. was the most important of the last ten years of his life. It would not be too much to say that it was mainly what kept him going. A third life, almost. Eddie first met Mark at the Edinburgh Science Festival on 18 April, 1998, after giving a talk on science and poetry, 'Poetry and Virtual Realities'.

Mark approached him to ask questions and talk about his own poetry. This meeting is recalled in 'After a Lecture' in *Love and a Life* (2003) and he also described the encounter in a letter to Richard Price (quoted by Jim McGonigal in *Beyond the Last Dragon*):

> Even from a few yards off I was hit by that old bolt, that coup de foudre, and I was shaking (like Sappho) as he began to talk to me. I never thought it would happen again at that age (seventy seven). But there it is. No rules in this life.

Mark was twenty-four years of age, dark, from Lanarkshire (like John Scott) and, as described by Jim McGonigal, 'gallus and sharp'. Mark wasn't gay, but as Eddie wrote to Richard Price in 2001—

> we've had quite an intense friendship for three years now. He knows my feelings ... and takes them in his stride ... he is very fit and physical ... what else? He has a sudden dazzling smile which makes you think all things are possible.

This intense and loving friendship sustained Eddie till the end. Mark stimulated him intellectually. He took over minding duties and accompanied Eddie on outings: for example, to a performance of his play *A.D.* in 2001; a birthday dinner at Mariscat in April 2002; to my friend Carmela's Tequila Evening in 2002 (up three flights of stairs!). And Eddie mentored and supported Mark in his studies, recognising and delighting in his energy and restlessness. My first impression of Mark was of an excitable puppy, eager to learn.

I spent some time with them both. We occasionally had lunch together. Mark was mischievous (a quality Eddie had too and must have seen in Mark) and was constantly teasing Eddie. He always called him 'Morgan'. He refused to call him by his first name. 'Morgan, what do you mean by that? Explain!' Mark would shout. But Eddie seemed to take it all in good part, was very patient (as love is).

One Sunday Mark decreed that we should meet him at a place called Oblomov on Great Western Road. I imagine it was the name that appealed, rather than the ambience. And he got Eddie and me to drink Bloody Marys, which neither of us had had before. Mark himself didn't drink; Eddie always kept a store of Fentimans soft drinks (Mark's favourite) in the house for him.

On 3 January 2001, the three of us had a new year gathering at Eddie's flat, with lots of fizz, mince pies and shortbread. We played a game Mark always loved: 'What's your favourite top ten films/books/singles?' It was great fun, swopping opinions and memories, but exhausting.

And on 6 October that year, there was another afternoon at Eddie's, this time with coffee and chocolate truffles and Eddie proudly displaying his lack of front tooth (it had come out on National Poetry Day). We engaged in the usual banter about films and books. Mark was a film buff, an expert on Italian cinema in particular and a fan of the Beats, as were Eddie and I.

Sometimes Eddie's friends worried that Mark might be too much for him, wear him out. Here was a new situation for us—what to do with a septuagenarian falling in love with a twenty-four-year-old! But in fact, Eddie loved it all. In 1999 he dedicated *Demon* to Mark (by name rather than initials, as was his custom), and the strength of the relationship is evident in the Mark poems in *Love and a Life* (2003).

13. Cancer All Round

In September 1998, my wife Winifred's father, Robert Walker, suffered a stroke and was rushed to the Victoria Infirmary on the south side of Glasgow. He never fully recovered, and died in February the following year.

I don't know if the stress of this triggered something in Winifred, but towards the end of 1998 she began to feel unwell and to suffer double vision. Opticians didn't seem to help and on Hogmanay she consulted an eye specialist at the same hospital. He quietly suggested she see a chest specialist. We didn't know what he meant. For the first time we cancelled our annual New Year's Eve get-together with Kevin McCarra and his wife Susan Stewart. This was most unusual for Winifred—she must have felt there was something badly wrong.

The very nice chest man thought she might have lung cancer. And so began a series of tests, with Winifred in and out of hospital, both the Victoria and the Southern General. The upshot was that she was diagnosed with terminal lung cancer which had already spread to her brain—a tumour was pressing on her optic nerve. By a strange coincidence, the final verdict was delivered to us by Jim McGonigal's daughter, Aileen, who was working as a neurologist at the Southern General. She dealt with us in an unforgettably kind and caring way.

Winifred's father died in the middle of these various tests. We'd managed to keep her illness from him. If I visited him by myself in the geriatric unit, I would make some excuse for Winifred not being there. After his death, she received a lovely note of condolence from Eddie.

In May 1999, she underwent a course of radiotherapy, which helped somewhat, and steroids eased the eye situation. As everyone does, we asked how long she might have to live. We were told months.

She was fifty-two. The children were devastated. I took early retirement (at fifty-one) from the library at the end of March. We cancelled our fortnight's holiday on Arran, but managed a few days in a luxury lodge there at the end of June.

Almost simultaneously, Eddie was diagnosed with terminal prostate cancer, although I gather there was some pussyfooting early on about the medics using the actual 'C' word—but

Eddie hated not knowing. Looking back as objectively as I can, it's interesting to compare the reactions of these two loved ones to their diagnoses. No thought of the dreadful 'bucket list' from either. Both were practical.

Winifred wanted to carry on as normal a life as possible—enjoying family, friends, cinema, books, television, meals out and as much music and singing as she could manage (she was a member of the Edinburgh Festival Chorus and sang in other choirs too). She had the furniture re-covered—even her piano stool. She sold most of her jewellery, and made sure the remaining three of us knew how to operate the washing machine.

Christina was still boarding during the week at Douglas Academy Music School and Kenny was working, so the house was relatively quiet. Winifred wanted me to carry on with literary stuff like Mariscat—*Demon* was in the pipeline—and continue meeting folk for lunch, etc. I now think she also wanted time to herself, to think and listen to music—a CD she played endlessly was Handel's oratorio *Saul,* a recording conducted by Charles Mackerras, one of her favourite conductors, under whose baton she had sung at the Edinburgh Festival.

The Chorus that year were performing Mahler's huge *Second Symphony.* Winifred went to rehearsals as long as she was physically able. We all travelled through to Edinburgh on 4 September to hear the concert and afterwards members of the Chorus came out to see Winifred and insisted we go back to Glasgow with them on their bus—a gesture that touched her.

Eddie was just as practical in his own way. He said to me after his own diagnosis, 'I know what I've got to do,' and what he meant was work. And work he did, producing three full collections, several extended sequences, and plays and translations. On top of that, treatments and clinics became a regular feature of life. He began a regime of Zoladex injections, at first monthly, then three-monthly: 'a huge syringe (the nurse said on Thursday it looked like an instrument of torture)', as he wrote to me.

There was palliative care for Winifred. Fluid retention was a constant problem; it tended to gather round her lungs and had to be drained regularly. I watched a session of this and there seemed to be gallons of the stuff, a liquid that looked like cider. Once, when we went to the Western Infirmary for the procedure, we were shown into the cancer ward, which seemed to be full of people crying out in pain. 'Is this what I've got to look forward to?' she said to me. There were also blood clinics to attend and a whole cocktail of drugs to be taken. A different life—but we got on with it. There was no choice.

Eddie asked my advice about what he should do, whom he should tell and when. I advised him to be more careful about what engagements he accepted. On 7 August, he wrote:

> I think you are right about those long-distance engage-ments, and I'll probably follow your advice with Moni-ack Mhor, and very likely Southampton and Leices-ter. I've always been so energetic that I hate to admit tiredness even to myself. But the warning on the box of tablets is clear: don't drive if you feel drowsy. I had the first of my quarterly injections today: a mighty jab in the stomach. I gave, I'm afraid, a little yelp. 'You have a tough stomach,' said the nurse. She warns me I may get hot flushes 'like the menopause'. Perhaps Winifred can tell me exactly what to expect, and whether there's anything I can do when it happens. —No more medical thoughts!—away! See you on the 15th.

Winifred and Eddie had interesting exchanges of symptoms. He also asked me to write to certain people explaining the situ-ation. In April 1999, he wrote to Winifred:

> Thank you so much for your card. I'm back to normal now, but the sciatica was very nasty while it lasted [and was to continue to plague him]. I've to go for an X-ray and blood test tomorrow—the doctor says 'Just in case'—whatever that means! I hope your leg contin-ues to improve.

And to me on 11 June:

> I expect to go to the SPL launch on the 18th assuming I survive the 16th, when I have a radiation scan at the Western (is that something Winifred had, I wonder?) [It was.] They inject radioactive material into a vein, then take photos with a gamma camera—just another 'diagnostic tool', they say, to pinpoint what's wrong.

Again, he wrote to me on 1 July:

> I'll be in London ... I'm splashing out on the Langham
> Hilton. I shall look on it as a counterweight to the
> news from Gartnavel [Hospital], which is not good. I
> had another thorough examination, from the profes-
> sor himself this time (and I must say the professorial
> finger was much more vigorous than that of his aco-
> lyte the last time round—I thought he was really at my
> innards). The thing is malignant all right, and the bone
> scan from the Western showed that the cancer has
> spread into the bone structure. I've to carry on with
> the tablets, and the injections start next week. Obvi-
> ously this is all control, not cure. But in a way, after
> months of uncertainty, it's a relief to know exactly
> what's wrong. One can lay out one's life, do the things
> that have to be done.

And on 17 July:

> Love to Winifred—I think about her. No hot flushes yet.

And on 30 July:

> I'm so sorry Winifred has been having further trou-
> ble with the lung—I hope things are clearing up now.
> My ultrasound session went (I assume) all right ... As
> I was lying naked on the table waiting for the probing
> to start, the young assistant doctor said, 'You wouldn't
> be Edwin Morgan the poet?' Hard to deny! I've told, by
> the way, Renee Rawlings [his cousin in Edinburgh].
> One old friend who ought to be told is Jim McGonigal.

Work on *Demon* progressed. Eddie returned his proofs on 25
June. He was also working on *A.D.*, his trilogy about Jesus. He
ended his covering letter:

> Have been writing poems, half a dozen. I've also fin-
> ished a prologue and first act of *A.D.* Act 2 is begin-
> ning to take shape in my mind, and I at least know
> what Acts 3-5 are going to be about. All this is before
> Jesus starts his ministry, so imagination is truly and
> I hope productively stretched. Wednesday is Urology
> day. Wish me well!

Demon was published on 9 August. Winifred helped me fold the dust wrappers for it on our dining-room table—the last time she would assist with Mariscat.

There was talk of her going into a hospice. On the afternoon of Sunday, 12 September I drove us to Pollok Park. We parked at Pollok House. Winifred managed the short walk to the river and we had a peaceful time just sitting by the water.

On 15 September at a visit to the Victoria Infirmary, her chest consultant told me gently she was 'winding down'. It was arranged that she would go in the next morning for another draining session. So we got up early. Winifred collapsed on the bedroom floor. I picked her up and carried her to the bed and she just went. The children were home at the time—and what a comfort and support they were.

Winifred hadn't wanted a funeral. She wanted her body given to the university for medical research, but we hadn't got round to organising it. Iona, her dedicated cancer nurse, said she'd investigate, but reported back to say sorry, they wouldn't accept someone who had had cancer. Which seemed strange to us.

So Winifred had a funeral after all, as low-key and simple as we could make it. My friend, John Young, a Congregationalist minister, agreed to conduct the service at the Cooperative funeral parlour in Shawlands. We played recordings of two of her favourite pieces of music—Miles Davis, *Sketches of Spain*, and Bach's *St John Passion*—and John gave the eulogy. Eddie was late arriving, because his taxi driver couldn't find the place, and he sat at the back. I turned round at one point and saw he was crying.

In a letter to me after Eddie himself died, my sister-in-law, Sheena, said she remembered being struck at Winifred's funeral by 'his obvious compassion and sincerity.' A week later he took Kenny, Christina and me to lunch at the *Ubiquitous Chip* in the west end—a kindly act. Two months later, I organised a memorial concert for Winifred at *Adelaides* in Glasgow, which Eddie couldn't attend but at which Jim McGonigal read the poem 'Fountain' on his behalf.

It's hard nowadays to find anyone who hasn't been touched by cancer in one way or another. For me and my family, it was a whole decade. Within a few years, the wife of my oldest friend

Leslie died of liver cancer. Then Michael Schmidt, Eddie's Carcanet publisher, was diagnosed with prostate cancer but was successfully treated. In 2008, I myself was diagnosed with prostate cancer. Luckily it was caught early. I had my prostate removed on 27 January 2009 and have been cancer-free since.

On 22 January, I received my one and only email message from Eddie (address, appropriately: morganedwin@rocket-mail.com):

> Still getting used to email [he never did] ... Good luck for the 27th!

My brother was also diagnosed with prostate cancer, and successfully treated at almost the same time as me (it often happens with brothers, apparently). But what a strange coincidence—Eddie, followed by his English, then his Scottish publisher, with the same disease. Prostate cancer is a killer. Michael and I are among the lucky ones. Eddie not so fortunate, although he beat the six years' prognosis by five.

And he kept writing up to 2005, despite all the intermittent treatments, clinics, hospital stays: that was his work. Writing his poems, of course, but there were also regular health reports. For instance:

> Yesterday I had almost the whole day at the Western. I went for my quarterly checkup with Kirk [whom we nicknamed 'Captain'], and told him about the reappearance of Darth Sciatica (told him also about needing a rail to climb stairs, etc). He's a wee bit worried about the sciatica, which may or may not be connected with the cancer, and sent me in the afternoon to get an M.R.I. scan (maybe Winifred had one of these?)' [Yes, and so did I.]

On a postcard in March, Eddie reported advance warning from Captain Kirk about the MRI, and his own impressions.

> 'Not painful but very claustrophobic', [Kirk] said. Indeed it was quite like being in a coffin, with a panic button provided. However, all was well ... I think on Saturday I shall not object to a large glass of wine. Love and Magnetic Resonance Imaging—Eddie

I remember, in the first year of his cancer diagnosis, walking with Eddie from his flat on Great Western Road towards Gartnavel General where he was due for some tests. I asked if he would like me to go with him into the hospital. He said 'No thanks' and I watched him trudge up the path to the entrance, a solitary, indomitable figure.

Tears came into my eyes.

14. Minding Eddie

I East

Eddie loved Glasgow but was also an inveterate traveller—overseas: Russia, Holland, Iceland, Hungary, New Zealand, America, Ireland, Albania; and all over Britain. He didn't drive and didn't like the faff of organising transport but that didn't stop him navigating trains and planes and buses (the last of these his favourite mode of travel).

His postcards always noted any delays, breakdowns, unscheduled stops, etc. A glance at his post-retirement timetable is enough to induce exhaustion—he seemed tireless and indeed had a tremendous energy and appetite for visiting schools (state and private), universities, societies and the like, reading and giving talks. The solitary writer, living on his own, could easily manage this.

So the diagnosis in 1999 of terminal cancer was a blow, both physically and psychologically, and over the next few years, try as he might, he just wasn't able to carry on as before. I advised him to cut down on engagements. At first he didn't want to tell people why, but he soon became more explicit. He was still determined to do what he could, and if an invitation was for somewhere not too far away (i.e. within reach of hospital or doctor), he would accept.

He commented to me a few times, in a kind of rueful, surprised way, on the diminution of his energy. He still felt he *should* be able to do things. He began asking me to accompany him to various events, sometimes to readings as his publisher, sometimes to occasions as a friend.

An early expedition, in July 2000, was to Edinburgh, that (to Eddie) inferior city. The occasion was his award of an honorary doctorate from Heriot-Watt University. We were put up the night before the event in the grand Prestonfield House Hotel (peacocks in the grounds) and attended a dinner at the university for the graduands, guests and staff. I sat between some chap who extolled the merits of corporal punishment and a former director of the Edinburgh International Festival who told us the story of how he went to Bayreuth as a schoolboy and lived on oranges and Wagner.

Next morning Eddie, in his modest way, wanted to have breakfast in his room, so I joined him there for a frugal meal of Rice Krispies, toast and tea, foregoing the delights of the dining-room. The chaffeur-driven car picked us up and took us to the Festival Theatre for the degree ceremony. Eddie had also invited his cousins Renee and Jimmy Rawlings and the jazz musician Tommy Smith, with whom he'd collaborated on several projects. After the presentation, we all stood in an awkward line for an official photograph, then had lunch, and Eddie and I got the train back to Glasgow.

We were back in the east a couple of months later, when Eddie was invited to read at Haddington by the poet Brian Whittingham, who was writer-in-residence for the Lothians. We were promoting *Demon* at the time and it was a successful reading, both from Eddie's point of view, and mine for sales. Also, I imagine Eddie was tickled by the idea of three Glaswegians invading eastern 'county'.

We seemed to go east a lot. In February 2001 we attended the launch of the EPIC translation project at the Scottish Poetry Library, which included Eddie reading some of his translations.

For a few years I was involved with Survivors Poetry Scotland, an organisation founded by the poet Larry Butler for survivors of mental distress and of the mental health system, using poetry—workshops, readings, publications—to help combat their effects—creative well-being. I contributed workshops on memory and publishing. It was decided to hold a weekend event, dubbed The Gaithering, in June 2001, on the campus of Stirling University, with readings, workshops, talks, etc—and a ceilidh on the last night. I was asked if I could supply a band for the event.

I gathered together an eclectic bunch of friends I'd played with in the past (I'm a drummer) and some of their cronies, and thus the White Street Band was formed (named after the street where Val Thornton, our whistle player, lived). I got Eddie to take part in the event and he agreed to be a guest reader. I went with him to Stirling and sat in on his reading.

It was one of the best performances I have ever heard him give (and I've heard a lot). The nervous energy that fuelled his public appearances was, as they say, firing on all cylinders.

There was the usual cross-section of love poems, political poems, science fiction poems, but he seemed to put even more into them than normal—the audience was absolutely gripped. I think he had caught the spirit of the whole weekend, its positiveness and drive forward. And he was surviving.

Another of the outstanding events, to me at least, was the exhibition—again, in Edinburgh—at the Scottish National Portrait Gallery in October that same year. This was 'A Tribute to Edwin Morgan', a joint mixed-media installation/exhibition by the artist Steven Campbell and the photographer Ron O'Donnel—an amazing collection of portraits and responses to Eddie and his work. I think everyone's favourite was Ron's yellow wallpaper featuring the famous 'eddiespecs'.

Eddie and I went through for the press launch. Claudia and Hartmut were there too. I was thrilled to meet one of the famous 'Glasgow Boys' and we all had a good lunch after at the Magnum, where Eddie lamented the fact that he was having his front teeth extracted the following day.

Edinburgh again in November. Eddie was at the stage in his life when he was having to endure a seemingly endless number of 'tributes', honorary degrees and the like. The Edinburgh University academic Colin Nicholson had published a study of Eddie's work, *Edwin Morgan: Inventions of Modernity*. He was giving a lecture based on the book, with a celebratory reception in Eddie's honour afterwards.

Eddie declined to attend the lecture; he couldn't bear the thought of sitting listening to a lot of stuff about himself; so we timed our arrival for when we thought the talk would be over. But when we got there, it was still going on and we had to hang around the buffet area until Colin had finished speaking next door. We could hear laughter and applause—we thought, what's he saying? Then much milling about, after which we were glad to escape. I'm sure it was this night, on our way home, we spotted a comet from the train and watched its progress. (If so, it would have been Linear C/2000 WMI.)

In 2002, Eddie was invited by the *New Left Review* to give a talk on politics and Scotland in Edinburgh during the Festival Fringe, at the Stand Comedy Club in York Place. By this time he was becoming a little anxious about outings, especially to places that had stairs. His balance was deteriorating and he felt particularly vulnerable on steps. I was dispatched to the capital to check out the Stand (which was below street level) and count the steps. I seem to remember twenty-two. As long as Eddie knew in advance, was prepared and had someone with him, he was fine.

On the day of the event (14 August) I went over early to Eddie's flat to wait with him for someone to collect us and drive us to Edinburgh. This turned out to be John Kay, father of Jackie, the poet and novelist (and currently Scotland's Poet Laureate). He was the most delightful and companionable driver we could have wished for—a pleasure there and back on that so boring road. This was the first of several encounters I had with John, usually at a Jackie event—he and her mum were great supporters. Just after writing this, I heard from Jackie that he'd died, aged ninety-four. He was a great human being, who fought for the betterment of other human beings. I remember we all had a convivial lunch together in the cramped club dining room, with some terrible comedian blethering away in the next room.

Yet another Edinburgh visit, in September 2002, was with members of the Association for Scottish Literary Studies to the home of the great Scottish man of letters, David Daiches, to celebrate his ninetieth birthday. We came with good wishes and a poem by Eddie for the occasion specially commissioned by the ASLS. They had requested me to ask him—my friendship with Eddie was considered useful by many, and not infrequently presumed upon. Eddie read his poem and posed on the sofa for a photograph of two old literary codgers and we toasted the birthday boy (who, according to the poem, was 'coming on') with whisky and nibbled nibbles served by his daughter Jenni.

One of my final outings with Eddie was to Edinburgh again on a dark, wet January night in 2003. He had been invited by the Whisky Association of Scotland to give a reading at their headquarters in Leith. This turned out to be reasonably pleasant evening in the Association's gentleman's-club-type rooms— dinner with several vintage whiskies accompanying, followed by Eddie reading in front of a roaring fire. Mostly men there. I think we both found the whole affair slightly precious.

On Tuesday 28 March 2000, I accompanied Eddie to Dunoon where he was to give a reading to fourth and fifth year pupils at Dunoon Grammar School. We travelled by train from Glasgow to Gourock from where we took the ferry across the Clyde. The ferry was, of course, 'Saturn'. I still have a rather murky photograph of Eddie standing next to a lifebelt with the ship's name on it. In the cafeteria during the short crossing, over coffee and scones, I asked Eddie what he thought of the new translation of *Beowulf* by Seamus Heaney. There was a pause. 'Too Irish,' he said.

Eddie was collected at the pier by one of the English teachers and taken off to the school. I met my sister-in-law Sheena Walker (a solicitor in the town; my brother-in-law Robin taught maths at the grammar school) and we went for lunch to the café in the lovely Benmore Gardens just outside Dunoon. The highlight of the gardens for me is the magnificent avenue of giant sequoias. Sheena ran me back to the ferry, in time to see Eddie being driven down the pier to the gangway. 'Saturn' again, back to Gourock.

I asked him how the reading had gone. Very well, he said. He had read a bit of everything—love poems, sound poems, science fiction poems, the 'Beasts of Scotland' sequence (apparently, and curiously, 'Midge' goes down better with adult audiences, he said) and Glasgow poems. He was asked the usual questions: how much is inspiration/imagination/reality; how do you get published; how much are you paid, etc. He had been given a cup of coffee and that was it. No lunch.

On the return train journey from Gourock to Glasgow we passed a warehouse near Hillington which had the sign SCOTTISH GALVANISERS above it. 'Ah,' said Eddie, 'that's what we need.'

Ah, I thought, we have one.

15. Lunches, etc

After Winifred died I began to have lunch with Eddie more regularly, in fact once a week, unless holidays or events intervened. These were a welcome distraction for both of us. Lunches for the lonely? A rough count from my diaries tells me we lunched together over a hundred and thirty times between January 2000 and June 2003, just before he went into Lynedoch Care Home. That's a lot of lunches—almost one a week for three years!

The original idea was to try a different place each week—which we did to begin with, but we soon found we had favourites and we tended to go back to them time and time again. We met sometimes in the west end but more often in central Glasgow.

We went many times to *Yes*, a modern restaurant at 22 West Nile Street, and *78 St Vincent Street*, a converted bank. (They are both no longer as they were. *Yes* became an all-you-can-eat Chinese buffet and *78* a hamburger joint. Change rules.) We had other favourite haunts, notably the *Ubiquitous Chip* (where Eddie used to take a group of friends every Christmas for lunch as well) and *Cul de Sac* in Ashton Lane, off Byres Road in the west end.

Other restaurants we tried included: *Rogano* (which is Eddie's main publisher Michael Schmidt's favourite), *L'Ariosto*, *La Parmigiana*, *Oblomov*, *Gamba*, *The Corinthian*, *Pizza Express* (yes, he liked the occasional pizza), *Esca*, *the Mussel Inn*, *One Devonshire Gardens* (which was handy for Eddie), *Bon Gusto*, *D'Arcy's*, *October* (chosen no doubt for tenuous Russian link), *Loop*, *Bouzy Rouge*, *The Inn on the Green*, *Lang's*, *Gordon Yuille*, *Est Est Est* (very positive); also hotel restaurants, such as the Hilton and Radisson. Very often the choice was Eddie's. He liked ambience as well as food, especially if it was a bit different.

For instance, he'd spotted that the George Hotel in George Street had a top floor restaurant called *Windows*, which offered a roof-top view of the city—just the thing, we thought.

It turned out to be less than exciting—although he'd been really looking forward to it. In order to view the hotly anticipated roofscape, we had to climb out of one of the eponymous windows and crowd on to a tiny balcony to see ... not a lot. And the food was fairly ordinary too.

More successful was the old North British Hotel beside Queen Street Station in George Square, now the Millennium Hotel. The refurbished hostelry had added a kind of conservatory, in which you could dine and look out onto the square— very appealing to Eddie's people-watching propensity. Of course, passers-by could see us too.

Eddie and I began this odyssey of lunches by each paying for both meals on alternate weeks. This was fine until one day, at *L'Ariosto* in West Nile Street, when it was my turn to pay, I found we had racked up a bill of over £50.00. After this I suggested we just split the bill and he agreed.

78 St Vincent Street became Eddie's second favourite restaurant. It was a vast space, with a mezzanine floor, dark wooden booths, linen tablecloths and friendly staff.

His absolute top favourite, however, was *Yes*, a ground floor restaurant with a basement in a modern building in West Nile Street, and not just for the name alone, which embodied his general attitude to life. Here he could get food he liked—meat and potatoes, fish and chips—and pudding ('I'm a great trifle man,' he commented once after sampling Winifred's at our house). One of our touchstones was tiramisu, our favourite dessert. We tried it wherever we could, but reckoned *Yes*'s version was the best in town. Over the three years we lunched at *Yes* over forty times and thirty at *78*.

Eddie liked mainly traditional food but was willing on occasion to try different things (see 'My First Octopus'). He was willing to risk a curry, as in 1983 when we all went for a post-event meal at the *Ashoka* in Sauchiehall Street—Eddie had just launched my anthology *Noise and Smoky Breath* at the Mitchell Library. I seem to recall that he picked somewhat unconvincingly at his dish.

The meal was notable, however, for another reason. Chris Carrell, director of the Third Eye Centre and co-publisher of the book, remarked, 'That was a good speech, Eddie, and we'd like to publish it for sale at the Centre. Could you let me have the text?'

Eddie muttered that he didn't always write out the text of a talk but would do his best. At ten o'clock the next morning he was in the Third Eye with a perfectly typed copy of what he'd said the previous evening. He was always reliable.

Simple fare appealed to him. I met him once (17 April 1986) in the *Rimini* near Charing Cross to give him the proofs of *From the Video Box* to check. I was on my break from the library and I ordered a cheese toastie. Eddie had apparently never come across such a thing before. 'I must remember that,' he said. 'That's the sort of thing I like.'

In January 1999, after an event in Gilmorehill Hall at Glasgow University to install stained glass windows incorporating lines from Eddie's 'Ten Theatre Poems', he wrote:

> The buffet was cold nibbles and a glass of wine. I thought they might have stretched to hot sausages on sticks, for a winter's night. (That's something I'm very partial to!)

Eddie liked food but he didn't really cook. He did have Katharine Whitehorn's *How to Survive in the Kitchen* and Bee Nilson's *Penguin Cookery Book* on his kitchen shelf, but he confessed that the latter was a present from a well-meaning friend. He could boil an egg, and make toast, and open a tin. The lunches I had at his flat were delicious and nicely presented, but mostly assembled from tins—even the potatoes.

He ended one letter to me saying he was just off to open a tin of Baxter's Cream of Asparagus Soup. He was once asked to supply a recipe for a celebrity cookery book. His 'recipe' was for an oatcake and marmalade inside a morning roll for breakfast. As he said (in 'On a Train'), 'What's life without a crunch?'

We were both fond of KitKat biscuits and of dark chocolate. We got excited when Nestlé brought out a dark chocolate version of KitKat. We had serious discussions about it and how difficult it was to obtain—forget literary matters!

In his English Department days Eddie ate at the staff club in the university. In his 1972 article, 'Notes on the poet's working day', he describes winding down, round about midnight, reading the *Dictionary of the Older Scottish Tongue* 'over a sip of whisky and a nibble of shortbread.'

In restaurants I noticed that after his plate had been served, Eddie always attacked his food with his knife and fork in a kind of chopping and mixing motion, which I imagine went back to his childhood, when many of our eating habits are fixed. He was also a 'penciller', that is, he held his knife in his right hand like a pencil, probably as his parents had held theirs.

Eddie and I communicated with each other mainly by letter and postcard. Neither of us liked using the phone. At our lunches we didn't have deep meaningful conversations. We talked about what we'd been doing, books we were reading, films and television programmes we'd seen, some literary gossip (he *did* relish some of that)—just ordinary chat. There was lots of laughter. These were friendly lunch breaks from other business: for Eddie a break from writing poems, publishing, editing, giving readings and talks, constant cancer treatment, travels when he could. For me, it was respite from writing, publishing, editing, having lunch with other people, the aftermath of bereavement. And much unspoken, no doubt.

Sometimes friends from both sides would join us, which is how I met poet Andrew Greig for the first time. He and his wife Lesley are now good friends, and Andrew and I play music together now and then (he's a good banjo player). Others who lunched with us included the poet and mutual friend Richard Price, Claudia Kraszkiewicz and her husband Hartmut Salmen (who set up the Edwin Morgan website), and of course, Eddie's friend Mark.

After these lunches I would usually walk Eddie to his bus stop or taxi rank. There would be the occasional encounter in the street. 'I seen you on the telly!' one youth accosted Eddie in Buchanan Street. Eddie, of course, was always happy to stop and chat. On these short walks we once noticed raised dots on the pavement at junctions. In our naivety we wondered what they were. It was a while before we discovered they were for blind people to indicate a road crossing.

We were greeted as regulars at our favourite haunts. I've often wondered if the staff knew Eddie was a literary celebrity. On one occasion, Jane Forrest and I were meeting him at *Yes* for a pre-Christmas lunch. When we arrived, he was standing disconsolately outside. 'They're fully booked,' he said. 'Right,' said Jane and she marched in and demanded, 'Do you know who you've turned away?'

We got a table and had a very nice lunch. Eddie himself would never play the 'do you know who I am?' game.

G12 0BG 3 11 1994

Dear Hamish

Yes, I think you probably ought to see RESERVOIR DOGS, nasty but gripping. I was there with my film pal Andy, who had seen it before and decided I must take it on board. The main interest (apart from special effects) is, What distinguishes the psychopath from the hardman? — a dividing-line that seemed to go blurry at times. The audience laughed at the final bloodbath, which shows there was something wrong somewhere. But as Andy reminded me, there are more violent films available on video. Ridiculous my not immediately recognizing Kenny — sometimes this happens when you see someone in an unexpected context, and my mind was swirling with images of the film. Well, I suppose it's PULP FICTION next, then NATURAL BORN KILLERS, then what! THE MONSTER OF FLORENCE (who serially killed loving couples and fried their genitals for supper)? Wouldn't it be nice to be nice?

12 November for a Manscat dinner would be fine. When shall I toil at the gin?

Best
Eddie

GLASGOW'S **78 St VINCENT** FINEST

R E S T A U R A N T · F O O D & W I N

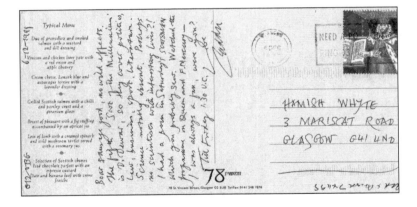

Typical Menu

Duo of gravadlax and smoked
salmon with a mustard
and dill dressing

Venison and chicken liver pâté with
a red onion and
apple chutney

Cream cheese, Lanark blue and
asparagus terrine with a
lavender dressing

Grilled Scottish salmon with a chilli
and parsley crust and a
geranium glaze

Breast of pheasant with a fig stuffing
accompanied by an apricot jus

Loin of lamb with a creamed spinach
and wild mushroom tartlet served
with a rosemary jus

Selection of Scottish cheeses
Iced chocolate parfait with an
espresso custard
Date and banana loaf with crème
fraîche

78 St VINCENT

78 St Vincent Street, Glasgow G3 5UB Tel/Fax: 0141 248 7878

HAMISH WHYTE
3 MARISCAT ROAD
GLASGOW G41 4ND

16. Diana

In the spring of 2002, Diana Hendry, the poet and children's writer, who had recently moved from Bristol to Edinburgh (after a stint as writer in residence at Dumfries and Galloway Royal Infirmary), sent Mariscat a batch of poems. These were her translations into English of Peter Hately Waddell's Scots versions of the Psalms together with her own poetic responses. She had seen a copy of Eddie's *Demon* and liked the look of it, so thought she'd try Mariscat with her new work.

I liked both the versions and her responses, and passed them to my friend and former colleague from the library, Joe Fisher (who was a theologically minded kind of person) for a second opinion. 'You've got something there,' he said.

I wrote to Diana to say we were interested. We met briefly at the Edinburgh Book Festival in August when I told her there was a letter in the post; and again on 19 October at the Scottish Poetry Library where I was taking part in their series called 'Selected Works'—a wonderful event, where speakers are invited to blether about their favourite poems. She and I had a chat after the talk, discovering a common interest in George Oppen, and arranged to meet on the 30th at the Elephant House on George IV Bridge to talk about her poems and possible publication.

On the day of our meeting, I was late. The train from Crossmyloof to Central Station didn't turn up. I rushed up to Shawlands, got a taxi and just caught an Edinburgh train from Queen Street at the last moment. I was out of breath from running up the Mound when I arrived at the Elephant House and didn't see Diana. Then she called my name from a table in a far corner.

Just two things to mention here. Firstly, I set the typescript of her poems on fire, by knocking them into the lit candle on the table (I eventually managed to smother the flames); and secondly, we fell in love. And, reader, I did publish the poems: *Twelve Lilts: Psalms & Responses* (2003), with cover illustrations by the printmaker Barbara Robertson.

And so it was that Diana was drawn into the Mariscat and Morgan circle. She came to the launch of *Cathures* in November 2002 in Borders bookshop (where she had her own book launch the following year). On 7 December she and I had lunch with Eddie at his favourite *Yes,* when he shyly handed over the typescript of *Love and a Life.* Diana later wrote a poem about this for his ninetieth birthday (in his own Cathurian stanza form):

> Today you're ninety and I wonder if you remember
>   that lunch we had at *Yes*?
> The Glasgow restaurant's name seemed just right for
>   a poet so poetically dauntless
> as you. That day, excited and nervous you arrived with
>   the whole ms
> of *Love and a Life.* Fifty poems typed on your Blue
>   Bird with barely a Tippex that—was it before
>   starters or after pudding—you gave to Hamish
>   of Mariscat Press.
> Such a slim folder! Full of more love and life
>   than anyone there could guess.
>   Eddie, you did us proud.
>   Here's happy birthday, laldy loud
> From Glasgow to Mercury and the other way round,
>   here's wishing you many returns of happiness.

I remember taking the bundle of *Love and a Life* poems back with Diana to her Edinburgh home and we sat up late, at least till 2 a.m., reading them, laughing and crying over the revelations. (I foolishly revealed this to *Guardian* journalist Sarah Crown when she came up from London in 2008 to interview Eddie and it got into her report—embarrassing, but so what?)

Eddie was still living in his flat at this time, but increasingly prey to falling. Jim McGonigal and I tried to make things easier and safer for him in the flat. Diana had the idea of a weekly home-delivery of groceries from a local supermarket. She organised this, which saved him from worrying about shopping.

Eddie visited Diana and me in Edinburgh just once, on 3 May 2003, for lunch. This was after viewing the Fabergé exhibition at the Queen's Gallery at Holyrood, which Eddie had been keen to see. Coming away from the Gallery, he was caught short and had to go for a pee just behind the building site of the new parliament. I did think of it as a kind of baptism for the new seat of government! He managed to climb the steps to Diana's house in the Stockbridge Colonies and we gave him lunch: quiche and wine. Diana was pleased he'd made the effort to come but also anxious. We hoped he was giving his seal of approval to our new relationship. He probably was—until I flitted. Diana has suffered an enduring sense of guilt at having taken me away from Glasgow and further away from Eddie.

After more than a year of shuttling between Glasgow and Edinburgh, I decided to move to the capital and share Diana's house. It was a big thing, to sell the family home—the children were not too happy about it, but they'd moved away to forge their own lives. I wanted—needed—a change, to rebuild my life—a second life, indeed.

By this time (early 2004) Eddie had moved into Lynedoch House, his care home in Bearsden on the outskirts of Glasgow, where Jim McGonigal and I could visit and continue seeing to his needs. The day I went to tell Eddie that I was moving to Edinburgh is one I won't forget. I can still see him standing in his bright yellow-painted room—and the look in his eyes when I gave him the news. Sad and distant, suddenly faraway. He said nothing.

It was heartbreaking.

By early 2003, Eddie was succumbing to more frequent falls and an inability to get up. In August/September he had a spell of three weeks in hospital after falling on the way to a check-up—he was kept in for observation and tests.

When I visited him in hospital—he understandably chafed against being there—he would talk about the other men in the ward, particularly the one in the bed opposite who would sign off every night with the words, 'Another day, another dollar.' Eddie became slightly obsessed by this phrase and asked me to find out its origin.

This proved more difficult than anticipated. Surely an ex-librarian could find the origin of a phrase or saying? The best I came up with was that it might be to do with daily payment of convicts in American prisons—another day over but at least there's a dollar earned. And this seemed kind of appropriate. However, by the power of Google I now find it's a phrase dating back to the 1850s, when it was 'more days, more dollars' and referred to sailors' pay. By 1907, it had morphed into the modern version and was popular with soldiers in World War I, when it had come to mean 'same old same old' (yet another idiom).

As James McGonigal says in *Beyond the Last Dragon*, it was clear to us that Eddie's situation required action. We tried to make the flat safer. Jim organised a walk-in shower. Diana arranged weekly deliveries with a local supermarket. However, we felt he needed more permanent care. He didn't want to leave the flat—the obvious solution was live-in care. But that wouldn't do: he just couldn't work with someone else in the flat, he wouldn't hear of it. And carers coming in and out regularly would probably be worse.

We talked it over with him. His group of friends talked it over among themselves. We all talked it round and round and round, and came to the conclusion that a residential care home was the best solution. After long discussions with him, he finally agreed.

Together with a friend and former colleague, Carmela Vezza, I investigated some care homes in the west of the city. We would walk in and tell the story of Glasgow's Poet Laureate who was having to move, and could we look round. There were some really gloomy places. The likeliest seemed to be Clarence Court, a custom-built residence on Crow Road at Broomhill Cross, not that far from Eddie's Anniesland flat. We thought it had a good atmosphere and caring staff.

However, Eddie was determined to go to Lynedoch House in Bearsden, mainly because he remembered visiting a retired colleague there, and seeing him sitting at a large book-covered table. And so he entered this Gormenghastly building on 4 October 2003. He was allocated a large, bright, ground floor room with a view towards Glasgow, the university tower visible in the distance, though the windows were quite high. Diana brought him a plant, Tillandsia cyanosa (Pink Quill)—which he noted in his notebook at the end of the manuscript of *Gorgo and Beau*, November 2003.

He was there long enough to write some good poems and be appointed Scotland's Makar or National Poet Laureate, with the official ceremony conducted in the grand hall of the building.

But it was suddenly announced that the home would close on 15 July 2004 (it was sold to developers). Almost immediately Jim drove to Clarence Court and managed to secure a double room on the ground floor for Eddie (occupied previously by a couple who had since died). It was a much more suitable location for him, back in the city, with a view this time of the street and tenements.

Jim and I divided tasks between us. Jim looked after day-to-day things and I attended to buying books and stationery—especially the black box files for his correspondence—and paying in cheques at the Clydesdale Bank. I had by this time moved to Edinburgh and wasn't any longer close at hand. Eddie came to rely heavily on Jim.

After Eddie had moved into Clarence Court (Room 12), it was easier to visit than Bearsden. I would get a train from Edinburgh to Queen Street, take the Subway from Buchanan Street, get off at Partick and walk along Dumbarton Road, then turn right up Crow Road. There was a florist's on the way where I sometimes got him a bunch of flowers or a pot plant.

Some visits 2005/2007 (written up from my diary)

9 June 2005

Took Eddie his Lord Provost's Award for Literature 2004, which I'd received on his behalf the previous evening at a dinner in the City Chambers (arrived about twenty past four). The nurse who let me in asked, 'Come to see the professor? He's just back.' 'Just back?' I echoed. 'But he never goes anywhere.' 'They've been on an outing to the Museum of Flight at East Fortune,' I was informed.

Eddie at his desk as usual. Told him I'd heard about the outing. The bus was very hot, he said, & the museum not very interesting, unless you're fascinated by aeroplanes—but there was a Concorde there. He'd told everyone he'd flown on it. I told Eddie about *my* Concorde experience: seeing it flying overhead one day in Bearsden. Agreed it was a beautiful shape.

I gave him the Provost's Award. 'Ah, it's an actual object.' He looked at it, baffled. 'What am I going to do with it?'

We chatted about his teeth. He's having four extracted next Thursday. He's not sure what will happen—it'll mean he'll have no teeth in his lower jaw.

He gave me his old copy of J. H. Prynne's *Collected Poems*—he'd bought the new one (the residual academic, keeping up? or does he just have to keep up anyway?). Talked about the difficulties of Prynne's poems. No, he said, never mind about meaning, just read them, go with them.

EM asked me to send him some first class stamps. He looked at the clock. 'Is that quarter to five? We have to be in the dining-room by ten to.'

So I left. Passing the dining room I saw some of the old ladies already there. A touch of the institutionals. [He eventually gave up on the dining-room and had his meals in his room.]

15 August 2005

Eddie's growing a beard. He cut himself shaving & the blood took a long time to stop. He's on warfarin, so decided to give up shaving.

Had coffee with Janice [Galloway] who kindly ran me in the pouring rain to Clarence Court. Came in unannounced & Eddie looked put out—he likes to know when anyone's coming. He was in the middle of going through a fat folder (poems? correspondence?). But soon thawed. His beard's growing nicely. Took some photographs of new beard & gave him a copy of Ron Selliman's *Under Albany* which he'd ordered. He thinks Selliman one of the best of the L-A-N-G-U-A-G-E poets. Discussed EM's forthcoming Carcanet collection, *A Book of Lives*, & roughed out list of contents.

EM agreed to collaborate on a series of found poems based on Edgar Rice Burroughs's *The Cave Girl* (1913)—a book he read as a boy—using the copy I'd found in a church sale in Coldingham on holiday & had sent him. Trying to keep some poetic juices flowing! [The results appeared as 'Wild Cuts' in *A Book of Lives*. Eddie's are the pieces with 'Too Many' in the titles. We had fun doing it, passing it to and fro between us.]

On his desk a photo of his young friend Asha [a teacher from Edinburgh who visited and sometimes took him out in her car] & her husband Arthur, taken on their wedding day at Zennor (W.S. Graham country).

Mark phoned to say Eddie not so good. The cancer has spread to his right leg & painkillers not working—& he'd had a fall.

After meeting Alan Riach at the Uni, walked down to Clarence Court. EM in a lot of pain, but doctor coming tomorrow & may give him stronger painkillers. He's had next Beatson oncology appointment moved to 3 Nov.

Eddie in a bit of a flap about forms sent from Andrew Motion's Poetry Archive. (I took them to deal with.)

Also anxious when he couldn't find latest poems for our Burroughs collaboration—but they were in a folder under the desk.

He can't walk & has to use a wheelchair and be assisted by two people to the loo. 'A bottle for Number One, & I buzz for Number Two!'

EM gave me ms of Munchausen poems [to use in my seminar on editing his work for Glasgow University Scottish Literature students]. Chatted about his working methods: the thinking ahead in his head, the writing quickly, how few revisions.

6 January 2006

Saw Eddie p.m. Seemed a lot better, but left leg swollen round ankle. Talked about his Gilgamesh play & a possible performance by Nat. Theatre of Scotland. I rabbited on about my paper for forthcoming Burns Conference. Jim [McGonigal] arrived with new dressing gown for Eddie—his red one got lost in the laundry (common occurrence), but since turned up. EM now has *three* dressing gowns!

11 May 2006

Saw Eddie in the morning. He asked if I'd come about 'the letter'. Says he's had a bout of depression & had written to Jim about it [Jim never received it, if in fact he did write it]. Said I didn't know anything about it. Talked a bit about depression. He said they weren't giving him drugs—the answer was 'character'. Gradually the old Eddie came out to play & we did a lively 'interview' for *The Big Issue* (they'd asked him for a piece about 'home'). A good visit. He said he was writing 'something.'

3 July 2006

Took [poet] Brian Whittingham with me. We'd been to a preview of refurbished Kelvingrove Museum—able to tell Eddie about it & show him photos on Brian's phone. Brian talked about recent visit to Lithuania & asked Eddie if he had a favourite place from his travels. Eddie immediately said, 'Istanbul—the colour, the smells, the boats, always something going on.' Another good visit, Eddie quite lively.

25 July 2006

Eddie slightly distant. Hard to tell if because I hadn't been in for a while or something else. I'd brought a speaking clock for him—tap it, it tells the time. [He'd grown confused about a.m. and p.m.] EM agreed to try it out [as he agreed to try all gadgets we brought him—he generally resisted them and they would end up in a drawer or lie unused].

27 February 2007

A Book of Lives launched in dining room of Clarence Court, with smallish gathering of about 25 friends, publishers & fellow writers. Eddie hoped to read something & had practised, but still pretty frail after recent strokes & it was a struggle. Others read for him. An amusing photograph [it was published in *The Herald*] taken, all of us hiding our faces behind the book except Eddie. A pleasant affair, with refreshments put on by the home, though Eddie would have liked a bigger splash. [He got this a month later at Kelvingrove Art Gallery for the launch of *Beyond the Sun*, his series of poems on paintings in Scottish collections. I was there and it was a huge crowd, milling round him, queuing to have books signed. I worried he'd become exhausted, but he loved it all, a smiling centre of attention he hadn't had for a while. We can be too careful sometimes.]

29 July 2007

Visited Eddie with Robyn Marsack—mainly to tell him about forthcoming Aye Write Festival's 'Big Read' next year. Plan is to ask around for people's favourite Morgan poems & publish them as *From Saturn to Glasgow: 50 Favourite Poems by Edwin Morgan.* Glasgow City Council will give away 10,000 free copies through libraries, galleries, bookshops, schools, etc.

'What a daft idea!' he said.

12 December 2007

'Poetry—a thrilling adventure into language, not policed—it's for everybody or it's for nobody.'

18. A Dog Called Eddie

The last visit in my diary was 25 June 2010, when I visited with Jim McGonigal, but I saw Eddie in early August, when he asked me to reply to a letter he'd received. The letter was from Sean Ashley who was involved with the campaign to stop Trump International building a golf resort at Balmedie near Aberdeen. He was asking Eddie, as 'one of our greatest and widely acclaimed Scottish poets', if he could lend what help he could to the campaign by contacting the Tripping Up Trump website. Eddie told me he remembered a quotation, which he thought might have been by MacDiarmid but wasn't sure, about Scotland being 'home of a million golf balls.'

I wrote to Mr Ashley on 11 August to say that, although pretty lively, Eddie was unable to correspond personally; he had read the letter and wished to let him know that he was anti-Trump; he was not online in the cyber sense, so couldn't access the website, but I assured him that he was very much online in other matters. And relayed Eddie's quotation but said we couldn't remember the source. That was the last time I saw him. And I see the letter is more optimistic about Eddie than his actual situation merited.

Jim was called to the home on the evening of Wednesday 18 August. A persistent lung infection was causing Eddie distress in breathing. Jim tried to call me but I was out. He emailed at ten to eleven to say Clarence Court had phoned and that Eddie was really struggling to throw off the chest infection he'd had for a week—the doctor had been called. Jim found Eddie weak and not really focussing.

There was some discussion about whether to send him to hospital but the doctor felt sure the hospital couldn't do much more for him than Clarence Court. Jim had seen Eddie the previous Saturday when he'd been quite confused by a visit to the eye clinic earlier in the week and seemed pleased to be back in familiar surroundings. It was agreed that he be nursed in his own room. He was given antibiotics and something for the fluid on his lungs and a small dose of diamorphine to calm him and help him rest.

Jim wrote: 'The doctor seemed very competent and caring. We'll see if he manages to recover strength. But staff seem very concerned about the outlook, I must say. I'll see him tomorrow and let you know.' As Jim recounts in his biography, they talked of poets and poetry before he slept.

Eddie died the next morning at 9.45 a.m.

Jim registered the death the following day. On the death certificate Eddie's occupation is given as 'Poet'. The cause of death was I (a) Bronchopneumonia (b) Primary prostate carcinoma II Congestive cardiac failure / Cerebrovascular disease.

We had a meeting that same day at Glasgow University to arrange the funeral and make lists of people to contact. Then Jim and myself, and poet and academic David Kinloch (recently appointed as another executor), went to the well-known Glasgow firm of undertakers Wylie & Lochhead (who had arranged Eddie's parents' funerals). Here Daniel Macrae helped us choose a simple coffin and organise the newspaper announcement. All this kept us busy for a week.

On 26th August, the morning of the funeral, I walked along the road from our house to the tiny community garden next to the Falshaw Bridge over the Water of Leith (not Lethe) and cut a thistle head from the huge plant growing there. The funeral and celebration were to be held in the Bute Hall of the University of Glasgow. When we arrived there I placed the thistle on Eddie's coffin.

Jim has described the funeral in his biography but I'd like to add a few more details. Jim himself read Eddie's translation (from 1962) of Yuri Pankratov's poem 'Slow Song'. My daughter Christina sang the Beatles' song 'Here There and Everywhere'. (She had trouble finding an accompanist at such short notice but managed eventually to enlist Frikki Walker.) The Rev. Stuart MacQuarrie (the University Chaplain) said in his opening address this was Christina's 'tribute to someone who was a huge inspiration and influence on her life.' I read 'Love' from *Love and a Life*. Jackie Kay read 'From a City Balcony'. Liz Lochhead read Eddie's favourite 'Cinquevalli', and David Kinloch read 'Strawberries'. Robyn Marsack of the Scottish Poetry Library gave the eulogy.

A choir of students and graduates of the university, specially formed for the occasion under the leadership of student Katy Cooper, sang Robert Burns's 'Is There For Honest Poverty' and we all joined in singing 'A man's a man for a' that'. At the end we processed out to 'Strawberry Fields Forever', played on the magnificent Bute Hall organ by John Butt.

A small group of friends went with the coffin to the Maryhill Crematorium for final goodbyes. Malcolm and Mark spoke movingly of Eddie, and Diana particularly remembers Malcolm as 'raw with grief'. We returned to the University Chapel where Glenmorangie (Eddie's favourite tipple) and Tunnock's shortbread had been laid on for guests. I have a family connection with Tunnock's. They were customers of my father's firm, which supplied them with cocoa butter to make their famous Caramel Wafers and Teacakes. When Winifred and I got married, Tom Tunnock baked our wedding cake as a present. So, a pleasing connection—not to mention the infamous Tunnock's Tee shirt Eddie wore to the Scottish Poetry Library on his eighty-ninth birthday. We had remembered that midnight sip of whisky and nibble of shortbread from 1972 when it came to the funeral purvey.

I got several warm letters of condolence. Willie Gilfedder wrote: 'Thanks for the note about Eddie, we were great pals for many years. Good luck!' Janice Galloway, the novelist, who was at the funeral, emailed:

> So sad to have missed out on a hug today, but I did not sit with the 'family and close friends' since I felt I did not qualify and that's where you were. It was a superbly genuine and moving event and I'm sure you've not had much sleep preparing. Not one apologetic speech, not one dud poem. Obviously. It must have been a hard, hard day for you. I could have done with giving you a hug. I did get to hug Robyn who shone like a star. She always does. It's the quiet ones who knock you out.

The day after Eddie died Mary Marquis, the broadcaster, wrote to me:

> As you probably knew Eddie better than anyone, I know you'll have a heavy heart today, although despite the sadness, I do feel that the flashing meteor of Eddie's mind will now be exploring immortality to his own satisfaction—'caught up in another life'. In his poetry he leaves so many pointers to ways of dealing with loss

and grief. I think of 'The Second Life' and 'Resurrections', to mention only two.... No need to tell you that Eddie Morgan is irreplaceable, both as a unique voice in poetry and as an extraordinary man, but perhaps you'll take some comfort in knowing how very much your long friendship, warm affection and tremendous support truly meant to him.

On 27 August Jim and I went to the BBC building in Glasgow and recorded an interview about Eddie's life and work with Paul Kobrak to be broadcast on Radio 4's 'Last Words' programme.

To honour and celebrate Eddie, Nick Barley, director of the Edinburgh International Book Festival, put on a hastily organised tribute on 30 August. It was introduced by Richard Holloway, with a huge cast of friends and fellow poets reading his poems and saying a few words, preceded by two short films about him.

The readings were as follows: Tam Dean Burn, 'The Drum'; Ron Butlin, 'From the Domain of Arnheim'; Douglas Dunn, 'The First Men on Mercury'; Kathleen Jamie, 'Trio'; myself, 'A Gull'; Robert Crawford, 'The Loch Ness Monster's Song'; Tommy Smith, 'Wolf' (with sax solo, as at the funeral); Liz Lochhead, 'Cinquevalli'; Alan Spence, 'A View of Things'; Jackie Kay, 'Strawberries'; David Kinloch, 'John 1 & 2'; Don Paterson, 'From the Video Box 25'; Gavin Wallace, 'Rules for Dwarf-Throwing'; Janice Galloway, 'Scan Day' & 'Skeleton Day'; Andrew Greig, 'Jack London in Heaven'; James Robertson, 'The Summons'.

In the first two weeks of September, Jim and I cleared Eddie's room at Clarence Court, dividing stuff up for either the Mitchell Library or Glasgow University Library. Jim made a list of books on his desk. We found a drawer full of Eddie's spectacles in their cases. Whenever he got a new pair, he tended to keep the previous pair—a habit I have myself (and others, I suspect). I kept a couple of pairs—which later proved useful for exhibition purposes. I also took back the tiny radio I had given him and which he had never used. At least it was easier than clearing his flat had been. After discussion between the executors and friends, we decided to scatter Eddie's ashes in Cathkin Braes, that iconic place in his life and work. On 31 October 2010, Jim picked me up at Queen Street Station and we drove to Cathkin Braes. There were five of us gathered there at 11.30 a.m.: Jim, David Kinloch and myself (three of Eddie's executors), as well as friends Mark S. and Malcolm ('M.T.').

As we were about to scatter the ashes in the running water of a burn that we hoped ran down into the Clyde, a woman with a dog walked past on the path behind us. We were all convinced she had called the dog 'Eddie'. Mark ran after her to find out, but came back to say that we must have misheard—its name *wasn't* Eddie. What a pity, we thought—that would have been spookily appropriate. But it was interesting that we all heard the same thing. And amusing, too, we felt—we needed the light relief.

Mark emptied the container of ashes into the burn and we toasted Eddie in whisky or water. I had thought a toast was in order but had no Glenmorangie (which would have been most appropriate) in the house, so brought a small bottle of Highland Park instead. Then, as Jim writes in his biography, we all drove back to the city, dropping Malcolm off on the way.

Strangely enough, in the street where I live now in Stockbridge, Edinburgh, there is a dog called Eddie, a terrier. Eddie is a dog that likes the company of at least one person and howls if left alone. He is a very vocal dog. He is walked several times daily by his owner or other dog walkers and I see him trotting past almost every day. He must be the most walked dog in Edinburgh.

18. Epilogue: Typing the Poems

For Eddie's centenary in 2020, the Edinburgh publisher Polygon, by agreement with Carcanet, brought out five 'Morgan Twenties', booklets containing twenty poems and each on a different subject: love, Scotland, people, animals and science fiction/concrete poems, and each introduced by a different writer: Jackie Kay, Ali Smith, Liz Lochhead, Michael Rosen, Ken MacLeod.

I compiled these with the assistance of Robyn Marsack (who had the original idea) and James McGonigal. To prepare the poems for publication, I typed them out, ready to be sent to the typesetter. I know what it's like to type my own work—you see things you hadn't noticed, they can look different on the page. Typing out someone else's poems in bulk I experienced something similar but far more fascinating—and intimate: a glimpse into the other person's creative processes. There were quite a few typos too, I have to confess. The eye can lie.

I considered myself to be a close friend of Eddie's, though now I'm not sure how close. Eddie compartmentalised, like many do. I don't really know how close anyone was, or was allowed to be, to Eddie—even his lovers, who at least had the most physical intimacy. I asked him once if he showed or gave the poems he wrote about his lovers to the person in question and he said no—which I found strange. How could one not? He published them in magazines and books—he gave them to the world, but not to the people most involved.

My most physically intimate moment with Eddie was in his last years. I was visiting him after he had had a spell in hospital and he asked me if I would dress his bad bed sores. I hesitate to write this, this private and humbling moment of trust. But I treasure it.

Typing his poems in some ways was *more* intimate, almost intrusive. I was able to see the twists and turns, the use of banal phrases to say extraordinary things, the unabashed repetitions ('not', 'half', 'brisk', 'second', 'bright', 'shriek', etc) that revealed his obsessions. In a recent *Times Literary Supplement* letter, a writer (Van Ess) was quoted on the subject of the dramatist John Ford: 'literary identity is often also a matter of repetition'.

I felt I was getting an inkling of how Eddie's mind worked, its constant questions, its restless, relentless optimism about the future of humankind. I wondered why so many poems begin with a one-line sentence, and why so many lines end with particular words instead of beginning the next line with them (as would be more logical or expected), the wee connectives that face the empty white space to the right of the page: 'till', 'but', and 'and'

Acknowledgements

Partners are often last on the list of acknowledgements. Not this time. First of all, a loving thank you to Diana Hendry who has been the driving force behind this memoir—I'm glad she made me write it (and supplied the title). And heartfelt thanks also to my son Kenny and daughter Christina (not least for their memories), to Kate Hendry (for encouragement and questions), Kevin McCarra (for friendship and the fun we had in early Mariscat days), Robyn Marsack (for good advice), James McGonigal (for his friendship and his care for Eddie—and the biography), Frank Glynn (for more advice), Andrew Greig (for his epigraph), Lorraine Fannin and her wonderful house in Pittenweem where most of the memoir was drafted, Neil McCrindle (for transport), and Nell Nelson (so good to have a *proper* editor).

Earlier versions of two sections have been published as follows:

* 'Safaris I' as 'The Edwin Morgan Heritage Trail' in *The Dark Horse* 9/10, 2000. Thanks to the editor, Gerry Cambridge.

* 'Sustenance Provided: the bibliographical Morgan' in *Scottish Literary Review* 4:2, Autumn/Winter 2012. Thanks to the editors, Margery Palmer McCulloch and Sarah M. Dunnigan.

An extract appeared in *The Dark Horse*, September 2020. Thanks to the editor, Gerry Cambridge.

An article about writing the memoir, 'What about Morgan and me?', was published in *Gutter* August 2020. Thanks to editor, Henry Bell.

The memoir should be read in conjunction with the biography by James McGonigal, *Beyond the Last Dragon: A Life of Edwin Morgan* (Dingwall: Sandstone Press, 2nd edition 2012). Thanks to Jim McGonigal for permission to quote from it.

Correspondence quoted from in the memoir is currently in possession of the author but will eventually be deposited in the Edwin Morgan Collection, Special Collections, Glasgow University Library.

Special thanks are due to the Edwin Morgan Estate and the Edwin Morgan Trust for permission to quote from Edwin Morgan's correspondence and poems, and to Michael Schmidt of Carcanet Press for his championing of Eddie's work.

Warm thanks to both Mary Marquis for permission to quote from her letter and Janice Galloway for permission to quote from her email.

For permission to reproduce photographs, many thanks go to Valerie Thornton, Hartmut Salmen, Kenny Whyte and Muna Whyte.

The copyright of photographs belongs, of course, to the photographers.

Also by Hamish Whyte:

Poetry

- *Now the Robin* (Happen*Stance*, 2018)
- *Things We Never Knew* (Shoestring Press, 2016)
- *Hannah, Are You Listening?* (Happen*Stance*, 2013)
- *The Unswung Axe* (Shoestring Press, 2012)
- *A Bird in the Hand* (Shoestring Press, 2008)
- *Window on the Garden* (essence press/Botanics Press, 2006)
- *Christmasses* (Vennel Press, 1998)
- *Siva in Lamlash* (minimal missive, 1991)
- *Rooms* (Aquila Press, 1986)
- *apple on an orange day* (Autolycus Press, 1973)

As editor

- Edwin Morgan, *Centenary Selected Poems* (Carcanet Press, 2020)
- Edwin Morgan, *Morgan Twenties* (Polygon, 2020)
- *Ten Poems About Robins* (Candlestick Press, 2018)
- *Scottish Cats: an anthology of poems* (Birlinn, 2013)
- *Eddie @ 90* (SPL/Mariscat Press, 2010). With Robyn Marsack
- *Kin: Scottish Poems about Family* (SPL/Polygon, 2009)
- *Poems United: A Commonwealth Anthology* (SPL/Black & White, 2007). With Diana Hendry
- *Unknown is Best: A Celebration of Edwin Morgan at Eighty* (SPL/ Mariscat Press, 2000). With Robyn Marsack
- *An Arran Anthology* (Mercat Press, 1997)
- *Mungo's Tongues: Glasgow Poems 1630-1990* (Mainstream, 1993)
- Edwin Morgan, *Nothing Not Giving Messages* (Polygon, 1990)
- *About Edwin Morgan* (Edinburgh University Press, 1990). With Robert Crawford
- *The Scottish Cat* (Aberdeen University Press, 1987)
- *Noise and Smoky Breath: an illustrated anthology of Glasgow poems 1900-1983* (Glasgow Libraries/Third Eye Centre, 1983)

About the Author

Hamish Whyte is a poet, editor, publisher and former librarian. He was born in 1947 near Glasgow, where he lived for many years before moving to Edinburgh in 2004. He runs the award-winning Mariscat Press, which has published the poetry of Edwin Morgan, Gael Turnbull, Janice Galloway, Jackie Kay, Douglas Dunn, Stewart Conn, Michael Longley, Brian McCabe, Dilys Rose, Alison Prince, Brian Whittingham, Jim Carruth, Christine De Luca, John Glenday, Lesley Glaister and Richie McCaffery, among many others.

He has reviewed crime fiction for *Scotland on Sunday* and literary magazines for *The Scotsman*; he has been an Honorary Research Fellow in Scottish Literature at the University of Glasgow; he was awarded a Robert Louis Stevenson Fellowship jointly with his partner, the poet and children's writer Diana Hendry; and is currently Secretary of the Edwin Morgan Trust and one of Edwin Morgan's literary executors. He is also Convener of Edinburgh's Shore Poets and plays drums in two bands, The Whole Shebang and Dekoy.